Emma Tennant

GIRLITUDE

A Memoir of the
50s and 60s

VINTAGE

TO JULIE

Published by Vintage 2000

2 4 6 8 10 9 7 5 3 1

Copyright © Emma Tennant 1999

First published in Great Britain in 1999 by
Jonathan Cape

Vintage
Random House, 20 Vauxhall Bridge Road,
London SW1V 2SA

Random House Australia (Pty) Limited
20 Alfred Street, Milsons Point, Sydney
New South Wales 2061, Australia

Random House New Zealand Limited
18 Poland Road, Glenfield,
Auckland 10, New Zealand

Random House (Pty) Limited
Endulini, 5A Jubilee Road, Parktown 2193,
South Africa

The Random House Group Limited Reg. No. 954009
www.randomhouse.co.uk

A CIP catalogue record for this book
is available from the British Library

ISBN 0 09 927399 3

Printed and bound in Great Britain by
Cox & Wyman Ltd, Reading, Berkshire

GIRLITUDE

Emma Tennant was born in London and spent her childhood in Scotland. Her novels include *The Bad Sister*, *Wild Nights*, *Faustine*, *Pemberley* and *Strangers*. She has three grown-up children and lives in West London.

To Natasha Fraser Cavassoni
with love

Contents

Illustrations

ONE

A Girl

Emma Tennant at No.13 Chester Terrace, 1955
(by Tony Armstrong-Jones)

Here I am, in a photograph taken in the summer of 1955, in silk tartan with pale blue bodice, black velvet straps and a bunch of artificial Parma violets pinned between bosom and chin. My hair is fiercely set, my expression imperious as I gaze into the lens of the diminutive figure destined (though he cannot know it) to be a participant in the first Royal divorce. I seem much older than my seventeen years. My neck and my earlobes, temporarily adorned with fake pearls, await the inherited parure of the noble family into which I am likely to marry. When aged, so my stoical expression appears to suggest, I shall gracefully yield the gems to the bride of the heir and retire to a dower house on a distant estate. Until then I shall have little more to occupy me than the planning of menus and the arrangements of the various charities with which I will be concerned. It doesn't occur to me, as my confident stance in the drawing-room of the house in Regent's Park confirms, that I need to follow this path if I am to succeed in life. The world gives every sign of being at my feet. I left school two years ago at the age of fifteen. I can do exactly what I choose. After I have 'come out', at a ball, that is, which will take place in a marquee put up behind the room in the photograph. All the arrangements are in hand, down to the flowers for the Ball. They will come from Glen, the house in Scotland where I lived as a child, and will be picked and laid in long boxes, to be sent down on the night train to St Pancras.

Here, on the morning of 27th June, John McCubbin will collect them and bring them to the terrace, miraculously still standing after the bombardments of the last war, that has at its midpoint my father and mother's house. The rooms will fill with the smell of syringa, lilac and lilies. To add an exotic touch, a pillar of dry ice has been ordered, which, giving off a cloud of white smoke, will be one of the wonders of the Ball. Other unknown quantities are likely to include my father's siblings – his mother Pamela's 'jewels', as she liked to label her children – Stephen, David and Clare.

Apart from summer visits to Glen (these silently dreaded by all concerned and never referred to afterwards), I had seen very little of my father's family since coming to London, attending St Paul's Girls' School and preparing – as I suppose it must have appeared to envious and dismissive schoolmates – for a life of privilege and pleasure. So I can only vaguely guess at the movements and domiciles of my aunt and uncles. Clare, almost sixty at the time of my Ball, has the disconcertingly wide lake of grease across her mouth which caused her to be referred to by irreverent young men at the few dances I had already attended, as 'Aunt Purple Lips'. She had, according to family lore, last accepted the attentions of an admirer, General 'Monkey' Morgan, during the war and had been expected to marry – this expectation having, however, been dashed by the General's terse rejection of my aunt. 'Let's face it, we've had it,' were apparently the words employed to end the romance; and perhaps unfairly, were in abundant use whenever her name – which had been for some time

Mrs James Montgomery Beck II after a third marriage to an American of an old family – came up. My father, even if he heard the cruel brush-off repeated, maintained his habitual silence on the subject of the 'Jewels' and their preferences and misdemeanours.

Clare, as I picked up in the course of the few family conversations which concerned her finances and her future, lived in a flat in Bayswater. She had run through her money, and there was never any suggestion that her circumstances would improve. So from an early age I determined I would never live in Bayswater – in my mind's eye the flat was dark and dingy. Added to this, tales were told of my aunt's refusal to admit even her own children, so greatly missing was any sense of maternal affection. Bayswater, whence Clare will issue, lips gleaming a deep magenta and mauve, to attend the coming-out dance of her loved brother Christopher's daughter, had become the place to which ageing and unsuccessful girls were consigned. Even Clare's young and beautiful daughter Diana had been turned away, when she came for a visit, by the witch of Bayswater.

David, my father's younger brother, must have been by the time of my official entry into the adult world a resident of the south of Spain, of Torremolinos, and, later, of Mijas in the hills above the sun-oil sea. He too has married more than once – and as he is not a girl (and does not suffer, in the words of my elder half-brother Colin, from 'A Girl's Trust: they never make any money') he will marry again, bringing further silences from my father when the subject of the dark, handsome and narrow-hipped brother is raised. David is strong, clever; the family legend is that he would land his private plane in a field in order to read the signposts and discover where he was and where he must be going. This story, which seemed to me when I was young to show great bravery and nonchalance ('cool' had not yet been invented) came later to demonstrate with embarrassing clarity the lack of direction in my uncle's life. Some of his movements had, it was true, been more in the nature of leaps than considered steps. Impulse lives in a purse, and my uncle loved to indulge it. The Gargoyle Club, as seedy and un-fashionable as my aunt's Bayswater flat by the time I asked someone to take me there in the summer of 1955, had been the night palace of this king of impetuosity. I wanted to see the mirrored ceiling and drink at the bar where so many rebels had drunk a toast to nonconformity, while being careful, in their choice of haunt, to conform. But the atmosphere caused and breathed by my uncle had dispersed by the time I got there. It would come to my Ball from the bars and nightclubs of Spain. Letters preceded his arrival; and my father, who would break his silence from time to time by humming a snatch of the Negro spiritual 'Nobody knows the trouble I seen', could be heard singing and humming in his dressing-room and as he walked down the stairs to the room you see in the photograph.

I would give an account of my youngest uncle, Stephen Tennant, at this point – his environs, as they say in the old-fashioned guides of the time; his climate, his altitude – if it were not for the fact that Stephen's existence was, at that stage in his life, as unmomentous as the sludge-grey river which flows at the bottom of the garden of Wilsford Manor, the house he transformed from stern Jacobean look-alike to Hollywood-on-Avon after the death of my grandmother Pamela. Did Stephen come up to my Ball on the Salisbury line, with his housekeeper, the devoted Mrs Ford? Did he leave from the platform where, in the war, on finding a stationary train packed with troops, he had showered them with bluebells? How did he arrive in our house on the night of the Ball? It is certain that a muff of gardenias was delivered on the day. I see the petals curl brown now, as I walk back along Chester Terrace, the music from an exhausted band still rending the air, to find the discarded muff with its white satin ribbon lying on a (hired) gilt chair in the hall. Were my uncle's gardenias a sign of his euphoria, not then known, in the family at least, by any medical term? Had he not insisted to my mother that he had enjoyed himself so much during the evening that he would order a gold lamé suit straight away tomorrow? But where he would order it from – or whether he would return with his usual speed to the downs and water meadows of Wiltshire with Mrs Ford – can never be ascertained. I remember his gold hair, and a chuckling, pink face with still the traces of beauty. But, as happens when remembering the dead, he is surrounded by a hush so intense that he seems unreal in retrospect. For now, the Ball, looked forward to by the girl in the photograph, has yet to take place. The sound of a car making an unsuccessful attempt to reverse into a space outside the house (probably John at the wheel) comes in through the open window.

Birds are singing in the park; and, far off, lions in the zoo roar. Or maybe it's just the traffic, going up and down Albany Street – where, on the night of the Ball, the inhabitants will be kept awake, as they will also be in Chester Terrace Mews, the narrow, cobbled alley behind the flat roof of the kitchen, the base of our marquee.

The house where we live is a kind of vertical village, with the squire and his wife – my parents – on the first floor, above the room where the camera of the young Antony Armstrong-Jones captures me by a table in front of an oval mirror; and below the quarters occupied by me, their elder daughter, and their two other children, along with May, who was nurse to my mother as a child and is now, as a result of diabetes and an amputated leg, prisoner in the high ground of No. 13 Chester Terrace. Confined to a wheelchair and able only to look down through the banisters and wait for my mother or John to come up with meals or conversation, May has also Betty my dog for company. When John or Agnes the cook comes up late at night and needs to walk along the passage leading to the final flight of stairs up to their outlying quarters, May is sometimes caught there by them. Then, she must back on her wheels into the night nursery – as the room she shares with my younger sister is known – or find herself trapped in the bathroom, the upper part of her body wedged against the door while they pass. May speaks to Agnes, but Agnes, who is Czech, has little to say in return. Her heavy trudge on the stairs, from the time I slept on May's floor to the year – at which I have just arrived – when I am positioned next to Agnes and John on the top floor in a larger bedroom, always seemed to express the solitude and exasperation of Agnes. She had one friend, Charlotte, who lived in the mews and knelt, as I saw it, each day by the inadequate light of the window there, mouth bristling with the pins she used to take up a hem or let out a gusset. Charlotte was Charlotte Havelka and Agnes was Agnes Kabicek and as they were both Czech each was the only friend the other had in the world. So I thought, at least, for I had no idea then, or indeed for many years, that John entered Agnes's room once the obstacle of May and her wheelchair had been navigated, and stayed there with her all night. Even when I also had to push my way past May on the landing to reach my new quarters in the cloudy summit of the house and lay on my bed dreaming of the next day (for I never saw further than that) it didn't occur to me that John, whom Agnes constantly shouted at in her exasperation, was her companion in sleep. (Sex was out of the question, being unknown to me then, and so not a part of any memory.)

The night of the Ball, for all the anxiety over rain and other meteorological disasters, has turned out clean and bright. The marquee, which symbolises the new surge of confidence – in money, in making money and in the continuing proliferation of money, which had recently appeared in an England still seen as 'post-war' – is tall and spacious. Huge vases of pink peonies stand on plinths, and in the rosy lighting they resemble the puffed-out bosoms of the women in their strapless gowns. A window cut in the side of the marquee has foliage pressed against a Perspex pane; and a stuffed owl, found somehow by my mother, is placed on a twig there to look in at those – like my new friend Henry Vyner – who will lose their fortunes before long, at gaming tables; and a few who will marry in the course of the summer (Philippa, with the white dress and the curiously mature face under stiff, dark hair). The band, Paul Adams and his ensemble, make a great wall of noise in the marquee. The stairs are thronging with people – May, who looks down from her eyrie to find Stephen, David or Clare will never discover them there. 'Something's gotta give,' croons the bandleader. My elder half-brother, bowing and smirking, brings in the guest who has brought unwanted attention and publicity to the family, Princess Margaret, sister of the Queen. People stand back, like Agnes and John on the upper landing, when May, coming at full speed from the night nursery, has failed to hear them and finds she cannot control her chair. Another crush forms by the door to the drawing-room. My brother's party goes in.

For all the discomfort at the sudden newsworthiness accorded to the family by this link with Royalty, there is little doubt on the night of the Ball that my father is going in for conspicuous consumption in a big way. The house and marquee are all the reporter from the *Sketch* could have hoped for; in this canton overlooking Regent's Park (itself the most self-satisfied and royally connected of parks) there is not only unlimited champagne but a whole floor of temporary lavatories constructed in the basement and a kitchen for serving a ball breakfast of kedgeree, bacon and eggs and strawberries and cream. The Fifties, in their attempt to echo the decade before

German bombs flattened so much of the city, have succeeded, in Chester Terrace; the war might never have happened. The prophecy, in the caption under the photograph, declares that Lady Glenconner will give a dance for her daughter on 27th June and has, despite austerity measures and shortages of both servants and luxury items, come true. It is only one of many balls of the season, of course: my plate has been heaped with oblongs of white cardboard since early spring, inviting me, a total stranger as I at first saw it, to dance in dripping Hampshire fields in May, to go night after night to the Hyde Park Hotel in July, and even to don the silk tartan for an evening of discreet foxtrot at Buckingham Palace at the height of it all. We are in a new England now, one that harks back to the Brideshead snobberies with a vengeance. For me, it is all meaningless and belongs to the time after leaving Scotland – a time when I yearned so for the hills and the house I had left that my daily trip to school, either by No. 27 bus or in my father's car with John at the wheel, was so misted with sadness that nothing could bring any cheer. Now, for all the friendships I have tried to make, I find I have as little interest, on the night of my début into a Society which knows itself ineradicably changed – and refuses to admit it – in the people here and their world as I had in the competing, inquisitive nature of the other girls at my London school.

It's hard to say where the decision on my father's part to splash out, has come from. I didn't know my grandfather, his father Eddy, who is fixed in my mind for ever in a picture at Glen, at the oars of a boat on the loch he made there, where the valley ends, a good-

11

natured Scottish country gentleman in the standard green fishing hat, a steep ravine behind him. Eddy, I knew, had a penchant for buying famous landmarks, such as Dryburgh Abbey or Stonehenge, and then presenting them to the nation. Had I perhaps, in my father's unconscious mind, become one of these: in my ball dress (not the silk tartan but a dress from Dior in Paris, scarlet organza with a rose in its foliage mid-stomach) – was I, while in the act of being presented to the world, now being given away? It was impossible to know, if this were indeed the case, what a gift was next expected to do. But these vague worries and presentiments did not of course affect me on the night of the Ball. Anxious as poor May on the floor above to find someone I could at least claim to know by sight, I roam the first floor of the house, hearing cries of delight at the pretty room, the flowers down from their northern beds resplendent in white vases, my father's pictures gleaming in his grandfather's frames. I stop by the oval mirror you have already seen in the photograph and I look in, at my reflection. A girl looks back – but this girl has already undergone a transmogrification since the photograph was taken. The hair is short and just cut by the fashionable hairdresser, René: freed of the formal look required of young women in those days I have – as I see for one heady instant – not only lost the regal air, the air of unwillingly assumed maturity that had come with the 'post-war' years, but have also grown down into my real age. With the added possibility – and here I linger, vain and tall, in my red dress by the half-table in the L-shaped room that leads to the new ballroom – that I have changed sex, and am now a boy. A short-haired, irreverent boy looks back at me; and as I stand still entranced by the loss of a great weight (the sheer womanliness of being a girl) I see behind me (for of the friends I've made so far not one has yet appeared) the gaunt and unwelcome face of my uncle from Spain. I am asked to dance, in arrogant tones which I dare not refuse. I see reflected in the mirror before me, as chance would have it, two people I know, one a young man from Oxford with a wide smile, Jimmy Skinner by name, as clever and funny as the young men I have met in the Season are pompous and cold, and a girl I had been at school with, lost and offended in the swirling crowd. I am swept away from them, to a still almost empty dance floor. My uncle, so thin under his evening attire that to dance with him is like embracing an entire skyscraper under scaffolding, guides me at speed over the temporary parquet with what seem to me to be hopelessly outdated steps. 'There's a small hotel,' sings Paul Adams at a bellow into his microphone. 'And there's a Wishing Well. I wish . . . that we were there together . . .' My uncle's grip on my waist in the scarlet organza dress tightens. I look up in desperation at his midnight chin; from the nose and mouth come a reek of stale brandy. People are crowding on to the dance floor now: my elder half-brother passes, dancing like an advertisement for dancing, beaming over the head of his partner at me: 'Well done . . . !'

But what have I done? I am whirled past the little window in the tent; the music stops; my uncle stops. In the gulf, the gap of resounding silence, only two seconds long, before the next bout of music, I find myself on a level with the foliage set behind the tiny pane. The eyes of the stuffed owl look back at me. And beyond the artificial window, in the darkness of the night, I know the seamstress Charlotte Havelka sits, in her room that doubles as workroom and sitting-room, in Chester Terrace Mews.

My mother had employed Charlotte as a maid, at the flat in Bryanston Square where she and my father lived during the war – when they were not at Glen, or, in the case of my father, away in Cairo working for SOE. Chester Terrace had been made un-inhabitable by the bombing; when the war ended, Charlotte was invited to move into the mews and continue her real work, as a seamstress. She 'ran up' for me, in that summer of 1955, a mauve linen dress, suitable for cocktail parties, or for the fork luncheons which I shall forever associate with a professional 'bringer-out' of girls in the Season, Lady St John of Bletso, whose own daughter Frances was memorably to have said of her by her mother, 'My Fanny's smoking.' Charlotte also made dresses of paper silk taffeta; one of these, patterned with oversized roses of a violent green, was to receive its death knell on encountering the contents of a coffee cup held by Noel Annan, Provost of King's College, Cambridge.

Charlotte, while measuring and pinning, knelt on the sparse carpet of the little house in the mews, a flood of muttered comments in Czech pouring from her lips. Her face was as white as the paper taffeta she was handed in a bolt, by my mother; and a musty smell, which can only be described as the smell of dryness, emanated from her. Her friendship with Agnes, whom she had met by chance and must have been delighted to find in the big house in Chester

Terrace, was one of opposites, for Agnes, who was large and red-faced, had oil and grease at her fingertips, the long hours in the kitchen seeming to summon a shining patina to her person. I don't know, on the night of the Ball, whether Agnes had invited Charlotte to join her, in the kitchen invaded by strangers unpacking glasses, pulling ice from boxes, laying out slabs of haddock for the ball breakfast kedgeree, but I doubt very much that the two compatriots spent the evening together. Charlotte, who had no hand in the construction of either my mother's ball dress (also from Dior in Paris) of pale blue, of what used to be known as an 'understated elegance', or mine, had no particular call to assist us in donning these dresses, which were easily fastened and almost indestructible, being built with whalebones and further strengthened with what appeared to be a beige baize stiffened with wire. She may well have left her mews house just before the Ball officially started – at ten, I think, or ten-thirty – and turned right, rather than left into Albany Street, then the known refuge of an uncaught murderer and often mentioned as such, though it was never out of bounds to any of us. Turning right would bring Charlotte to the noble arch and pillars of the entrance to Chester Terrace: and she might, in order to watch the arrival of the Royal guest, have stood a few steps down in the area of the house, so as to be as unobtrusive as possible. My father and mother certainly had to shiver on the front step – along with Colin, who would have explained the protocol of the occasion many times to them – and could not leave their posts until the black Daimler appeared and the

Princess stepped out, ready to be greeted. — I don't know, as I say, whether Charlotte Havelka did in fact round the corner into Chester Terrace, walk along the road which is unusual in that there are houses on one side only, the other side being bordered by a thin strip of grass and trees (here a strange man had recently exposed himself to my younger brother, and grandiose plans to build a bridge over the road for the Ball into the garden there had been abandoned). Beyond this strip was the main Park Road, and beyond that again Regent's Park itself, which would have been surrendering its last light at about the time my parents were obliged to stand on the doorstep and wait for the Royal limousine. The evening was cold and Charlotte must have feared that spots of rain would fall on my mother's dress. Encroaching darkness, anxiety at the prospect of rain and the desire not to offend may all have kept Charlotte at home that night. Further, the area steps to the house on which I have placed her in my imagination may have been impassable, due to the plumbing necessary for the temporary lavatories (a Gents, naturally) which had gone into the basement in preparation for the Ball.

The progress of the evening itself, after the opening dance with my uncle, comes to me in flashes and of these the most vivid must be my failure to secure the romantic episode for which I had ardently longed.

Rory McEwen was the third son of a wealthy

Borders landowner, the façade of whose eighteenth-century house, Marchmont, concealed the tensions of a Brideshead: Catholic, snobbish, with the pretensions of an old family (though in reality not so far from the *nouveau riche* Tennants as they might care to believe), and above all, or so it seemed to me, in that innocent first summer of the three ball dresses (the third being a puff of white net in which wreaths of pink roses, like mice hidden in the folds, writhed in their lairs on my bosom and behind as I danced), vain. The vanity of the McEwens, so it appeared to us at Glen, a structure of shamingly Victorian date and hence to be despised by any true country house owner, lay in their clearly noticeable lack of desire to invite any of us to their grand and frosty house, an hour's drive away in Berwickshire. For a time, the fact of being 'post-war' put any thoughts of entertaining or being entertained by such as the McEwens out of mind. I believe Agnes, who had only recently ceased cooking at Glen, had left a legacy of rabbit in every possible form: casserole, schnitzel, fricassee and plain stew. Possibly my parents, who in any case shrank from neighbourhood exchanges in Peeblesshire, felt this cuisine was far below the expectations of the well-born (she had the air of a marquise in *Les Liaisons dangereuses* but was known for her piety) Lady McEwen. Or perhaps the unspoken insults delivered to the architecture of the house made the prospect unappetising. My father had done all he could to cover up the ornate extravagances at Glen – the ceiling roses with their groaning grapes, the cornices as deep as layers on the most over-the-top wedding cake – but still, it was felt, guests such as the

McEwens would sense this vulgar detail and curl up their lips at it. There was as well, of course, the unpleasant suspicion that any invitation issued to this family would be turned down, causing the exhaustion of dreading an event which in any case would not occur. And if, for the reason that one of the 'children' – as the young were called right up to the time of marriage – should accept a tentatively offered invitation, there came the equally disagreeable realisation afterwards that no return visit had been suggested. Like Royalty, the McEwens made their own terms, saw their (frequently French) cousins and guests, and ignored us altogether.

I had had an example of the distance of the family when travelling up to Scotland on the night train. As we approached Galashiels, the station from which I would be collected by John and driven to Glen (undoubtedly in the eyes of the McEwens an over-'colourful' landscape, heather and hills, roughly traversed by brown burns, as far from the eighteenth-century sense of order as it was possible to be), I saw in the corridor the lank and desirable figure of Rory McEwen, gazing out of the window at the green and pleasant landscape, not so far from Duns, the local village for Marchmont. He had his guitar with him, and there was no sign of his younger brother, with whom he would tour the smart parties of Scotland and London singing the then unknown songs of the great blues hero, Leadbelly. The combination of Scottish good looks and deep Negro gruff: *Take that hamm-ah!* etcetera would resound in the marquees and drawing-rooms of the upper and middle classes, as the rich were then known; and not a girl amongst the kneeling, sitting, enraptured audience failed to fall in love with a McEwen on those occasions. Whether any were invited subsequently to March-mont was, for obvious reasons, very much on my mind. — In the train, despite the fact that we had met several times before, my experience of Rory was just as I had feared: I blurted out an invitation to Glen, and was rebuffed with a kind smile and the informa-tion that 'there are people coming to stay and I'm helping with them'. Some days later, when my infatuation had got the better of me, I rang from the basement telephone at Glen (black Bakelite receiver sticky from John's latest imperious call to Ray, the grocer in Innerleithen) only to find Rory McEwen as adamant as ever that he could not come to Glen, however often I invited him. This time, to make matters worse, the names of the guests to be entertained by his parents were let out – 'The Comte de Paris ... Isabelle de France...' There was no question of my being asked there, to meet these profoundly terrifying people. I didn't ring again; and now, the evening of the Ball, was the first time it could reasonably be said that I had this McEwen on my own territory. It was frustrating to catch a glimpse of the troubadour (for this was how the McEwen brothers presented themselves, and they did indeed have one song, deeply moving to me every time I heard them sing it, which concerned an undying love, in French naturally; a love which in *un grand lit carré* and decorated with periwinkles, would last right up to the *fin du monde*, the only trouble, as far as I was concerned, was its being a reminder of the French guests whose presence at

Marchmont had spoiled my last summer at Glen). — It was more than frustrating, while being whirled with dance steps every bit as vulgarly ornate as Glen itself, round the dance floor by my uncle, to glimpse Rory McEwen, if possible even more glamorous in appearance than before, being approached and talked to by a host of girls.

None of this, I suspect, was lost on John that evening. He darted, winking at me as he went, from group to group, tray of glasses in hand: both officious and absurd, he loved to play the fool; to send up our pretensions at having what Lady Lamington, a friend of my mother's, would call a 'proper' butler when it must be made clear to all that he was no such thing. (And he loved to announce Lady Lamington, on the occasions she came to lunch at our house, on the threshold of the drawing-room: 'Lady Lamington!' the very word seeming ridiculous as he uttered it, the many winks and suppressed laughs clearly visible behind her back as the hapless visitor was transformed, by the magic of John's cinema, into a Marx brothers creation, a dignified and silly Margaret Dumont.)

John was John McCubbin; he had been a fire engine driver in Glasgow before being taken on by my father as valet/driver and butler, a factotum I suppose it was called, though I never heard him referred to as such. I knew he had also been a ping-pong champion, and that his middle names, due to an ancient friendship between his father and a German, were Carl Rombach. I sat on the kitchen table not so many years before the Ball, while Agnes wielded the little glass pots, a new idea imported from 'abroad', of home-grown yoghurt, a fetish of my father's but not very successfully done. I asked John about his name, John Carl Rombach McCubbin; and with the timing of the comedian he had (presumably) always been, John on each occasion gave me different answers. Carl – a German spy – Roam back – Scottish ballad, and so on. That this shortish man with pointed chin and irrepressible laughter was a twin was never believed by my mother, though he announced the fact from time to time, solemnly. She didn't believe him because nothing John said was expected to be believed; and also because it would have been impossible to credit (a word he always used: 'I wouldn't *credit* it!') that there could be two of John McCubbin in the world. His harem (for, as I learned, also much later, John had an almost Quint-like power over the housekeeper at Glen when we went up there: he was a philanderer, deserting Agnes and her heavy soups with their shining halo of grease for a Scottish marriage in the dank, tiled basement there) was as improbable as his twinhood. Yet the sheer speed at which he drove my father's car, a company Bentley much resented by schoolmates when I arrived at the school gates as fast as a conjurer's trick, indicated a probability of doubling, of lies and truth so rapidly entwined that any amount of McCubbins could have been in both places at once and still deceived us into thinking there was no one there but him. — I knew, therefore, as the Ball warmed up and I danced with one partner after another, that John watched me and laughed, but with sympathy at my lack of the one dance I wanted. His winks increased as he approached the older guests, my parents and my grandmother's other 'jewels' amongst them.

He was right to be almost unable to contain his laughter: my aunt Clare did seem to exude a cross despair, perhaps due to the clinging chiffon dress splodged with pale flowers, which showed up her stocky figure and her absolute oppositeness from my mother, who was tall and long-limbed, with a Thirties look of portraits and sculptures of that era – and still, as was patently obvious, a young and attractive woman. Clare's beauty, so long trumpeted as the inheritance from her wistful mother, had begun to go blowsy. Her white cheeks had the consistency of marshmallow, her eyes, large and circled with kohl, looked like the tarnished stones found at the bottom of a box in an attic, and her slight form, so frequently photographed by Cecil Beaton and pored over in shops that sold prints of contemporary beauties, seemed to have shrunk to little more than the chiffon which clothed it. — John's laughter, increasing by the second as he served Clare's son Harold – the Lord Tennyson whose abandoned luggage, so large a part of my childhood mysteries at Glen, remained, as far as I know, unopened and not sent for throughout his lifetime – came to a choking fit as he rounded the table and placed the tray of champagne directly under the nose of my other uncle, Stephen. If they all saw his shaking frame, no dismissal or expression of displeasure came from my father, who, I secretly thought, saw why John laughed and had no intention of preventing him. Through all this, well observed by me as the family table was situated by the entrance to the ballroom, I danced wanly, hoping in vain for attention from the elusive McEwen.

When the Ball was nearly over and the dry ice had
long since stopped giving off its white smoke, I went
to walk outside in a dawn that seemed about to turn
to day but held back still, white as the fragments of
the artificial ice on a distant horizon and dark still in
the long terrace with its one side facing trees and a
deeper blackness. My companion was Henry Vyner
whose appearance went back two centuries, to the
dissolute gambler (as indeed he became, having inherited a famous Cistercian abbey in the north and
determined to throw it away). In the half-light
Henry's almost chinless, pudgy face looked up at
mine anxiously. He was my confidant, or so he
thought of himself perhaps with all girls, for none
could feel any romantic passion for him; and so,
almost lazily, I had come to confide in him without
thinking that he might be bored or even hurt by what
I had to disclose. Henry's fortune must have seemed
enough to protect him – though of course it was not.
I said I had wanted the lank guitarist to dance with
me just once: I meant, it goes without saying, that I
had wanted to dance with Rory McEwen all night.
How – apart from one stilted turn on the dance floor
– could he have overlooked me so? I told Henry I felt
that the reason for my neglect by this Catholic young
man whose indigence (for the McEwens had many
sons and had run through their money) was known
and respected, was the result of my reputation as an
heiress of ill-bred origins; and even, on this sad
occasion, the Ball itself, with its vulgar insistence on
money ostentatiously splashed out in a 'post-war'
world not accustomed to show.

'No,' replied Henry Vyner, who had as little idea as

I, I dare say, of my real prospects (which were that I would not have money) – and who was in any case saved from any lurking suspicion of being a fortune-hunter by reason of the existence of his own enormous wealth. No, Henry Vyner went on to say, the reason for Rory's lack of interest in me lay elsewhere. It was a fact, so he would tell it to me. And, as we walked down the road, with its white houses like ghosts (I believe they were none of them occupied then but were offices or left empty, property of the Crown), I saw us, as can happen in those eerie moments, the pair of us from far away: a shambling, roué of unprepossessing appearance but with a kindly, worried smile and a girl in a scarlet dress, the 'heiress' of the tabloid press but in reality no such thing. My hopes of conquering the heart of this distant Borderer were nil, it seemed. I was ready for anything – for, even as Henry spoke, I saw myself standing on the brink of a new life. 'Isa is Rory's girl,' said Henry drunkenly. 'Isa – he's in love with her.' And as my memory took me to the impossible rival – to the eternal love, the periwinkles, the sense that the one I wished for was in fact bound to a Dame *à la* Licorne, an impossible mythical figure who must always hold sway over his heart – my real self took me with a bound away into the future. But the wolves in the zoo found us that night as we walked back to the dying Ball and the house and they bayed as John came laughing out on to the front step.

MILLY THE DEB

An Interlude

I met Milly when she was brought over to our house in Scotland in the spring of the year of my Ball; and it became clear, before this daughter of a square-jawed Tory politician (knighted for his services but known, as someone pointed out shortly before the arrival of Milly, as Smartie Boots. 'Why?' I asked. 'To hide his hairy heels,' came the disconcerting reply), that Milly, pink-skinned and blue-eyed as she was, had fixed her sights on one McEwen if not two, and had also decided to conquer London by virtue of her handling of the Season in all its complexity.

'So when will you face the astonished multitudes?' was Milly's first question to me, as she climbed from the car and came to stand on the front doorstep at Glen, under the array of grinning stone gargoyles. 'Is it this year, or next?'

Before I could reply – it was hard to know whether an about-to-be débutante with the obvious ambitions of Milly would prefer competition or a declaration that she alone, of present company, would go before the people, as dauntingly described – Milly had intimated to me that we should walk in the garden and discuss the exciting times that lay ahead. For she had known all along, as I much later divined, that I was to 'come out' too, and the assumption of the brief summer being a 'marriage market' as outlined in the *Daily Express* and other interested journals had clearly been taken very much to heart. Of the lords and possible McEwens (these of course not rich but

27

socially desirable) on offer, would Milly carry off the most prestigious prize? Or would she, to the probable chagrin of Smartie Boots and his wife, exhausted from a round of dinners in Cadogan Square, 'end up' with a man with neither title nor guitar, a dim figure without Royal French connections to compensate for the lack of cash? Milly fixed me once again with a steely look (we were by now away from the 'grown-ups', as I still saw them), and we stood just by the stone plaque on the wall saying PAMELA: HER GARDEN, which led me to wonder what my deliberately unworldly grandmother would have thought of Milly's approach. 'I suppose the shooting here is good,' came the first salvo, 'but I gather one has to go north to enjoy the real thing. Stags and things, I mean. Are you doing the Highland balls this year – probably staying up at Cawdor? – you know Hugh, don't you? I hear he's quite sweet. By the way, another Hugh – do you know the Master of Reay – he lives quite near here, doesn't he?'

I couldn't give anything to Milly she didn't already know about the Hughs – and, as I suspected, the bone of contention for me – she also divined my tragic desire to lure a McEwen to Peeblesshire and my total failure to bring this about, and the increasing irritation on the part of my family at my public humbling of myself before the white-haired 'Marquise', Lady McEwen, which was shortly to be brought out into the open.

'We've just come from Marchmont,' Milly announced, waving at the gate to the driveway where the car, driven by an immensely hard-trying and thus ignorable young man, her escort for the day, was parked. 'I found Robin – well he is so clever, but I adore Rory, don't you? I do think Marchmont is such a heavenly house . . .'

And here, as in a parody of the cursory examination I had dreaded from my unattainable love, she looked up and squinted at the impossible château-of-the-Loire façade of the house I had grown up in and only slowly learned was to be despised by those who were well-born and endowed with their own impeccable architectural features. With a look of great pity, Milly directed her pale blue gaze at me. Mention of Marchmont, home of the Bourbon-worshipping Borderers, had brought a faint blush to her cheeks, and as she spoke she twisted daisies (we were now on the wooden bench directly under PAMELA: HER GARDEN) into a diadem which, with a glorious air of wealth and grandeur, she placed in a self-coronation on her head.

'Where are you going, to curtsy?' was Milly's next and if possible even more unanswerable ploy. 'I'm going to Madame Vacani's, aren't you? And – for a second I had thought this newly anointed queen demanded obeisance from me – she rose and walked to the steps up to the french windows of the drawing-room. The young man, blushing with pleasure, stepped out; with a great show of indifference Milly brushed past him and went in, to the drawing-room, the lights and the people – the beginnings, at least, of an astonished multitude.

I didn't learn to curtsy – indeed the matter was never discussed – but it so happened that the next time I saw Milly was at the one occasion where curtsying skills were *de rigueur*. This was

Buckingham Palace, at one of the last presentations at Court of débutantes; the custom of placing three ostrich feathers in the hair had already been discontinued, and, like the British Empire, the whole notion was going gradually down the drain. Milly showed no sign of having taken in the air of imperial exhaustion, however, and was quick to whisper to me, after we had queued in a stuffy ballroom and, one by one, stood a split second in front of the Royal Family on the dais, before dropping down to perform what looked, from the rear, very like the laying of an egg. 'Prince Philip smiled at me,' was hissed in my ear, after I, embarrassed and uncomfortable, had done my constipated-poultry turn in full view of the throne. Then, as I tried as discreetly as possible to find my way out, Milly seized my arm and guided me to a corner where a gilt chair with a cushion contained the tired but triumphant figure of the professional Presenter at Court, Lady St John of Bletso. It turned out Milly had been one of her charges. 'Isn't she *sweet*?' I was led away from the multi-chaperon at equally great speed and Milly took me over to the bar, where she seized a glass of champagne and pressed another into my hand. I could see she was nervously excited; perhaps there was an engagement in the air. 'I'm going to Ramsbury – not the house of course . . . .' Here she broke off and giggled. 'To stay with – oh, Patrick Lindsay and Christopher James – and I think – no, I'm sure of it – the McEwens will be there! What do you think I ought to wear?'

As was often the case with Milly, I didn't know what to say. I still pined for the troubadours from the north but – as the continuing lack of interest was making clear – I had few expectations of ever pleasing them. 'Wear?' I said. I wanted only to leave the Palace, and the refreshments were as unrefreshing as could be. Why on earth did Milly – she in pale blue watered silk for the occasion, I in cabbage green with a hat to match – worry about her clothes for the coming weekend? Surely, neither of us could ever look quite so silly again. 'I don't want to be – you know – over-dressed,' she said. 'Oh look, there's Prince Philip again – he's probably looking for me. I've heard the people at Ramsbury – well, you know – they play games after dinner . . .'

'Games?' My attention had wandered; I was desperate to leave. 'You mean bridge or canasta or something?'

'No, no –' Here Milly went a deep pink and let out a loud laugh. 'Rushing into – well, into girls' rooms – drenching them with water. That kind of thing.'

'Just wear what you're wearing now,' I said, knowing I was being cruel.

'Really – but if it's late –'

Milly's voice tailed off. A minute later she was gone: perhaps she had spotted Prince Philip in an unguarded moment and had run to him. I went home at last, and thought nothing more of Milly – except when Smartie Boots was in the papers, looking out with a determined smile which reminded me of Milly and her headlong attack on the Season.

I did hear, when the summer was over, of Milly's visit to the house in Ramsbury. Apparently there had indeed been 'games' after dinner and the girls' rooms had duly been raided by rowdy young men. I couldn't ascertain whether the McEwens had been amongst them. 'It was so ghastly when they came to Milly,' my confider told me – this was a man not entirely enamoured of the ambitious but undoubtedly pretty Milly. I asked, half dreading the answer, what had been found there. 'Milly was so obviously waiting for the raid,' my friend said, laughing. 'She was in her pyjamas –'

'Poor Milly, she probably got tired and wanted to go to bed.'

'Not really very likely The boys hosed her especially hard, as you can imagine. She had to let them pull off her pyjamas.'

'Oh God,' I said. No girl I'd met was more prim and proper than Milly; she had even, as I remembered, told me once she was 'saving' herself for her marriage – of course (though unspoken) to a lord.

'It turned out she had a thick set of underclothes on underneath,' my friend said. 'She was ready for anything, Milly.'

TWO

Banco

Colin Tennant and Emma Tennant in a
grouse butt at Glen, 1955

I am emerging from the church – or rather the chapel, the Grosvenor Chapel is its name – and my dress, though this cannot be seen in a black and white photograph, is gold. It's 'real gold', so Charlotte Havelka pronounces when she sees the garment, three-quarter length, long-sleeved but with the casual cut of what was then known as a 'shirtwaister': sculpted for me by a leading dressmaker, John Cavanagh, it may cause unintentional spite on Charlotte's part when I take it for her to see. From her dark mews house in the autumn of 1957 will come clothes less vital to the act of getting married than the wedding dress itself: a beige wool number (when it gets chilly on the Lebanese honeymoon this can be worn every night as dinner – always the same: *oeufs en gelée*, then chicken or pork – is brought to the silent and baffled young couple by the plate glass window in the George Hotel, Beirut that overlooks the sea); a navy coat and skirt (this the appellation for a suit, a word apparently not to be used, any more than 'costume' is permitted to describe the jacket and matching skirt which no young married – for such, in November, I will become – can be seen without); a raspberry tweed overcoat, with 'raglan' shoulders so sloping that my chin seems to slope into nothingness as well when I stand there for a fitting. I feel the panic of class, the trap of marriage: am I to be a housewife? An upper-class lady of leisure? The glowing pinkish tweed, found I am almost certain in the little mill by

Neidpath Castle in Peebles by my mother – or in the Porteous workrooms in Innerleithen, the nearest town to Glen and on the banks of the River Tweed after which it is named – brings me with a kick of further apprehension to the days when Scotland was all I knew as my home. From an upper window of the fake fortification my great-grandfather had put up a century earlier, to impress Mr Gladstone and the Whigs, I might watch the arrival of one young man or another who might become my husband. Or I might turn away, and by ignoring the visit, lose the proposal, the trip up the rainy valley to the loch, the glum realisation that neither had wanted this to happen, followed by the relief of freedom, and home to a late tea. Now I have the sense it is impossible to escape. What will become of the bolts of cloth, the pins on a little bright cushion, this probably brought by Charlotte all the way from Czechoslovakia before the war that separated even Agnes from her when a cook was needed for my safe house at Glen, away from the bombing? She'd had no one to cry with, as her country was lost to Hitler. The pins, an elite amongst them the possessors of little round glass hats, brightly coloured, will be taken from the evening dress and the raspberry coat, if I flee from my wedding on its appointed day. The clothes, half made, will lie in Charlotte's flat – a Miss Havisham scene – and worse, although I know my mother would pay her, Charlotte will refuse, her pride in her craft destroyed, the trousseau somehow responsible for my savage change of mind. I am as wedded now to the turquoise moiré (no Peebles provenance for this, a supplier of French silks, taffetas and moirés in

Bond Street which my mother and I have visited together has provided the exquisite material, with its look of an ancient book-binding, watermarks overlapping like a mermaid's tail that has been pulled from the sea) — as wedded as I shall shortly be, in Grosvenor Chapel, South Audley Street. What has happened, that has taken me from the Ball of two years ago – when I was a girl – to this impending stage of womanhood? Shall I be altered beyond recognition by the time 'we' (I must get used to the term) arrive at the Savoy for the reception my parents will give there for the wedding of two cousins (at least it's all the same family)? Will my father's siblings, such as the much-married Clare, greet me with a dreadful familiarity? And my elder half-brother Colin, who announced the year before at the time of his own marriage, that he would 'never make another joke' – was this a taste of what would happen to me?

As I look down at Charlotte's head – she has a bun of grey hair, a cat that smells, an electric fire which is by no means enough to heat the room in the little mews house – I fidget and show my impatience to be gone. Charlotte should be making me a cloak that would render me invisible, so this girl who will soon no longer be a girl can vanish and roam the world, quite free. 'You know, with that gold material,' Charlotte says indistinctly, still kneeling, her mouth full of pins, 'you have to take care.' She looks up at me, and tacks the hem of the beige wool dress that will cope with the sudden chill of the eastern Mediterranean in winter.

The pins return to their native cushion: we both

stare at the wedding dress, which lies in a white cardboard coffin on the floor. 'I make a pad for here, you know.' Under arm is indicated; Charlotte looks down again and the dry, musty smell from her mouth when she speaks hangs in the air. The gold dress will tarnish, so Charlotte says. I shall appear after the marriage ceremony green in the armpits like a coin made from a base alloy.

What had happened, in that brief spell, two years since the marquee built out on the kitchen roof, the disappointment in love, the boxes packed up next day, with Agnes shouting in her exasperation at John's quick friendship with caterers and his jokes at the expense of poor May, whose new nurserymaid Mary was due to arrive that day? ('He who hesitates are lost!' John calls out, as May, swerving to avoid him in her wheelchair on the landing, finds herself jammed once more in the nursery bathroom. Betty, the collie dog I have brought down from the Borders, barks and whines apprehensively. 'Go – and it went!' cries John, mimicking his reaction to a red light when approaching one at top speed in my father's Bentley. But he is kind really: Agnes's shrugging insistence that May's diet today must consist of ball leftovers (haddock encrusted in boulders of rice, hard-boiled egg green at the edges) is secretly undermined. He will personally cook and bring up a fresh meal – 'Egg-but-no-bacon', as he sang out to me each morning in the gloom of the dining-room before we set off for

school. Maybe, too, a punnet of strawberries, untouched by ball waiters. John has an uneasy
friendship with May, for all the complaining at
having to supply meals for her which Agnes can
reasonably voice.)

What, after all the excitement, and in the words of
my uncle Stephen, the 'grand success' of the Ball, has
led me, at the age of nineteen, to a hastily decided-on
future probably as much feared by the groom, a silent
and nervous young man, as myself? Why have I got
to go? What wolves, sensing my folly and ignorance
of the world, have dragged me to their lair? I had a
job – my father had insisted, wisely, on that – a job
that was the only one my lack of qualifications and
my position in the world appeared to be able to
produce, on a glossy magazine, as assistant in the
Fashion Room. (Perhaps, for the first time, the
consequences of my decision to leave school at fifteen
began to occur to me.) Yet I didn't 'share a flat with
another girl' – still fairly rare in those days; the
'career girl' hadn't yet been born. I didn't set off on
my own, to another part of the world – though I was
to do this later, when it was indeed too late. It seemed
(for nineteen was by no means considered young to
marry, then: my experiences since the Ball led me to
feel I was already on the shelf) that my only safe
course lay in imitating the lives of my parents; and in
staying near them. The wolves had taken away my
innocence and this could be restored through the
adopting of matronly ways: as a married woman I
would regain the privileges – now seemingly lost for
ever – of a girl. Girlitude – perhaps this is a term for
the dependence, the longed-for protection and the

self-reproach of a species which can now only be alluded to self-consciously and with scorn – was the formative experience then; and it didn't occur to many of us to look elsewhere for fulfilment or happiness.

The wolves in my case had been particularly strong-throated. Dominic Elwes – a member, like Rory McEwen, of an old Catholic family but otherwise bearing no resemblance to the pious Borderers with their love of the descendants of the court of Marie Antoinette – was the son of a Society painter, Simon Elwes. The fact that Simon Elwes had executed a portrait of my aunt Clare – this, finally transported to my younger brother's hill farm in Scotland, where it cannot fail to look out of place: huge, lurid, a monument to snobbery, chiffon and silk, a real 'drawing-room picture' – failed entirely to cut ice with my father. Dominic Elwes was Bad News. It was said of him that he was psychologically incapable of telling right from wrong. I can't remember what the term for this complaint was then, but my father certainly had no desire to learn it. My visits to nightclubs and to his Mount Street flat with Dominic brought an air of anger and reproof into the house – though I was as determined as ever to deny the existence of any disapproval of my behaviour. (My mother, too, looked askance: she feared for me, she went so far as to suggest I 'look after things' – that is, that I find the means of preventing a pregnancy, if this wolf in wolf's clothing should go ahead with his obvious intention of seducing me. But, at a time when a visit to one of the rare specialists in this area, a woman doctor who demands icily that I provide proof of my engagement, is the only way of following her advice, the prospect doesn't invite: like other members of my family, apart from my father, I disregard common sense and please myself.)

My father has other anxieties on his mind, in that summer of 1956. Suez brings a wave of shouting to the whole country: there is shouting in our dining-room too, and writer friends of my mother, who are more inclined to be leftish than my father, inspire badly suppressed outbursts of laughter from John as he circles the table. The Wilkie portrait on the dining-room wall, *The Spanish Girl*, looks gravely out at us from under her high comb and black lace mantilla, as Nasser is excoriated and the health of Anthony Eden, famously, begins to fail. Stephen Spender, Alan Ross, Cyril Connolly – I know only their faces when, after dinner and ensconced in the giltwood cherry-velvet-upholstered French chairs in the drawing-room above, John hands round Trinidad grapefruit juice from a tin rather than the brandy and liqueurs that might otherwise have been expected. My father has family interests, long ago inherited from his grandfather Sir Charles, in the West Indies and the grapefruit juice, tart and sour and arriving in oddly dented tins, shall be given to the guests however much they may crave – as some demonstrably did – something stronger.

On top of the aggravation of Suez must have been the fact of my eldest half-brother's willingness – at the age of nearly thirty – to join the family firm, C. Tennant Sons. All the family money, the house and estate at Glen, the aforementioned land in Trinidad – C. Tennant Sons is an import-export business – are due to pass down to Colin as a result of an entail formed by my father's father Eddy when such things were fashionable, an aping of the aristocracy to ensure that the continuing ownership of all such assets passes down for three generations to the eldest son. Now, some years after selling Constable's *Westminster Bridge* to 'a tractor king', as the press had it – this with the permission of our father, for, although the entail ends with Colin, my father is of course in 1956 still alive – it appears to be time, finally, to go into the family business. The boats and jetties and bustling river trade of the famous painting which had filled a whole wall in the Hall at Glen have paid for his life but now he needs to work (this, at least, is the view of May, as she sits, Player's cigarette in hand, staring down at the dark blue box of 100, with the bearded man on the lid). May's lips pucker as she remarks that this will be a difficult time, should my brother continue to arrive as he had on his first day at the offices of C. Tennant Sons at No. 4 Copthall Avenue in the City of London, with his pyjama bottoms showing under the trousers of his new suit. And we both laugh; for, despite my father's thunderous moods on his return through the Blackfriars Tunnel (often in the company of John McCubbin, whose laughter has entirely disappeared), we feel the intrinsic comedy of my elder half-brother: his vow to make no further jokes is seen, by my mother and myself, as well as May, as a joke, for how can this lightweight keep such a promise, even in the solemn circumstances in which he finds himself? Colin has recently married a girl with wheaten hair, the eldest of three daughters of

Lord Leicester, of Holkham Hall: they are known, say the wits of the Season dance floors, as the Norfolk Broads. Despite all this, we are none of us to laugh ever again.

Maybe it was the celebration of this marriage – from which I, as a girl, found myself so firmly excluded – that prompted me, not so long after, to choose myself to walk down the aisle of a sparsely attended chapel, in the chemical wedding dress (which would prove, as Charlotte had predicted, sensitive to my sweating armpits and turn a strange combination of mauve and green, a kind of verdigris, at my nervous reaction to matrimonial ties). There were other reasons, of course: the 'psychopath' – a friend of my mother's had rung with this new and regrettably exciting appellation for Dominic – had removed my girlhood and I was in line to walk the plank. But the pines, the great space of the Holkham beach I went across with Henry Vyner played their part: how sad we both look in the photograph, poor Henry like a puffin in his topper and I, sick at the slight which has been done me, sulking and plain in Charlotte's beige wool from the year before. — To my surprise, I, as sister of the groom, had been placed in the beamed house, stockbroker Tudor as such houses were known then, of a distant acquaintance of the bride's family. I must bang my head on the inauthentic wood, stumble on the *faux*-crooked stairs of this black-and-white nightmare set, like a house in a porno movie, in a straggly copse. Pines, like the mournful forests that covered Lord Leicester's estate right down to the sea, soughed in the vile summer weather, as the host plied us with Pimms No.1 and

pushed us round a refectory table as imitation Nell
Gwynn as the rest. Henry's presence permitted more
self-pity. I had not been invited to the Hall, in all its
architectural perfection. I was a half-sister, I was a
girl. I must queue, with tenants of the estate, to shake
hands with the bride's father (who later was to lose
his sanity and call for housemaids to stand on tables
to dust the tops of pictures so he could have the
pleasure of seeing right up their skirts). My mother,
who developed a migraine on the occasion, was
obliged, in the chapel on the Holkham estate, to
perch behind my father and his first wife Pamela, like
a heathen wife permitted to witness a Christian
service. This must have been my first taste of real
nobility. It was said of the Earl – like so many of his
kind in the landscape close to Sandringham, he was a
courtier (and given in his later years to the
unwelcome habit of telephoning the Queen Mother
and announcing he knew her to be in the bath,
soaping her breasts) – that he had given his eldest
daughter seven and sixpence as a wedding present. It
was hard to know whether this was indeed a
forbidden joke – or the truth. Certainly, Lady Anne,
the bride of my elder half-brother and with two
younger sisters as pale as the Holkham sand in the
chapel behind her, would receive nothing, not
Holkham or even seven and sixpence, when the old
Earl died. Everything would go to a distant male heir;
she had little choice, perhaps, other than to marry a
husband with money: she knew the extraordinary
situation, in her class (the class our kind of family
tried to copy) of being a girl.

An ancestor of Lord Leicester, who built the Hall

where I was not asked to stay, boasted that his nearest neighbour was the King of Denmark. I think of the great sands, the sea so far out you might never reach it, however hard you tried; the sudden galloping tide, the flight under pines. My brother and his new wife left the lawn of Holkham for their honeymoon, in a helicopter. Henry and I, I suppose, returned to London by train. For a time my father will emerge from the Blackfriars Tunnel after a day in the City with a calmer expression: he cannot abide the presence of his son in the office and his son can't bear him. John, grave as ever when he has accompanied my father back from work, by way of the underworld – or so my father's descriptions of the Tunnel and the traffic to be found there have come to make it resemble – is nevertheless ready to tease and laugh more quickly, with my brother on his wedding journey. The subject of this impossible paternal and filial partnership is never mentioned at home and it's as if the honeymoon might last for ever. It doesn't, of course, and my brother, whether or not he has cared to remove his pyjama bottoms from under his City suit (in this soon outdoing my uncle Stephen in eccentricity, in an age long before tailors let rip with their fantasies: suits with no pockets; suits made of an early scarlet PVC, suits of exotic fabrics from far-flung posts of the receding Empire – my brother ultimately pays the price of the tension between father and son and collapses, driving up to Scotland on the motorway.

These tensions may have contributed to the need I felt for escape, anything other than marriage to the slur-speeched lord who has presented himself, with his castle in the north (no longer habitable), as suitor in the first part of that year. I have no idea of living anywhere other than at home, and want to enjoy myself there – with friends who come for drinks when my parents are away (John, ecstatic with excitement, mixes Bourbon and cherries and orange and lemon slices and lumps of sugar soaked in angostura bitters: soon he has at least two men flat out on the floor) – and at the nightclubs and restaurants where Dominic and his friend Michael like to take me and flee as their cheques bounce in the hall. — My father tried to curb the drain on his finances and his temper by installing in my little sitting-room an antique cellarette which will contain three bottles a week, for my friends. But the visits to the cellar continued unchecked. One night Dominic, fresh faced, blue eyed (all the corruption and consequences of his life went into the swarthy and haggard features of his companion Michael) fell right down the steps into the basement and lay there as if dead. But, protected by his strange nature, he was up again in a moment, and only Michael and I showed in our faces the fear and shock of his fall.

It's hard to give the order of events in that year and in the following year, 1957, the year whose end saw me posing for Charlotte as she sketched around me, cigarette in hand, the folds and contours of the dresses and 'coats and skirts' which would take me from my pretence of being a girl to the reality of married woman. I know I went to France, to the farmhouse in the south near Valbonne which my father had bought as a young man. Here, released from the strictures of war into the Cézanne planes and colours my mother loved, there was one simple room for eating and sitting, primitive bedrooms and a terrace bordered by vines and lavender. Yellow butterflies flapped over the stone table; wasps, drawn to the sweet, thyme-scented honey of the Alpes Maritimes, rushed at the tears on my face as I stumbled back from the telephone in the hallway where my father's voice told me of the death of May. I think of the one friend out of a group of friends staying who saw the confusion – the first death of one close to me – of my last rush from the upper floors of 13 Chester Terrace and my own impatience at the prospect of missing the plane. I see, from May's angle in her wheelchair my head as it goes down the stairs, glimpsed between the bars of the banisters, and I hear 'I'm going into hospital next week, darling' and my own dismissive 'I know!' as I flee to the car. — So May, whose care for me went unregarded, will not be there when I return. — But when was it that we moved away, so that even her ghost would not be able to visit us? Was it that autumn or the following spring? The months have neither green nor falling leaves, as in old movies, to spell out the calendar of my disgrace: there was a Fall, but it was not that of the year's end, it was mine.

My father is in the drawing-room: certainly we are in Chester Terrace here, for the Meissen birds, their china plumage turned away from the spectator in the photograph, are facing outwards from the satinwood table against the wall and they are bright, turquoise and cherry red, exotic birds, worth, as I have heard, 'a lot'. (What this is I almost, fatally, discovered, for on a recent absence of my parents from London two

men, both of an almost ludicrously criminal appearance, had appeared at the door, talked their way into
the house and climbed the stairs, picking out the
Meissen birds in the drawing-room at once and
making me a series of offers. In the end, fool as I was,
I sold them a bracelet I was wearing. I dare say I was
short of cash, as usual; my suitor and his gaunt friend
would 'borrow' from me when they could.) My
father is sad, and stern: he informs me I am changed
and can never return to being the person I once was.
So – from this scene, with the unbearable brightness
of the birds as I stand a minute looking at them, and
then make my way with a heavy tread to the floor
above – I know I was still in our old home. I will
suffer the disapproving gaze of the 'family doctor' –
but this is a family after all, like other rich families in
decline, who call on the services of a magician, a
Viennese wizard with a love of powerful men, to
extricate them from their scandals and misdemeanours. — I will be told to go to Switzerland to
give birth. — I will refuse. So, alone and late at night,
a taxi will take me to Hendon: the obloquy, the
stirrups, nurses as cold and unforgiving as the Fates,
with their lost babies and broken wombs in the
washed-down operating theatre.

Now (where have the birds gone?) we are in
Chelsea by the river. I have been bad news; my father
and mother love me and are kind but I am ill, I suffer
and – at least one good thing – I have rid myself of the
Lochinvar from the wrong side of the loch: the wide-
grinned, narrow-trousered lover who has brought me
down. I know the need to regain the approval I have
lost. My job – at *Vogue*, carrying shoes in taxis, to

the demands of editor and photographer: my role as background, at the shoots in stately homes (Run! Run! called Parkinson, and I must do so, against the pale plasterwork of Osterley, the great marble stair-cases: later I will become a blur behind the models, a whole party suggested by my rubbed-out presence) – my job is gone and I have nowhere to go. Like the grand furniture taken on approval by Dominic in his flat (sometimes sold on, often recaptured by bailiffs) I no longer have a sense of my own permanence. I wish for approval – but I am on approval to myself. Any day I may be sent back, so I feel – but where? To the Girl Factory, I might reply today.

The world I inhabited for this brief time that seemed so long, between my Ball and my new attic in Swan Walk, with its neat view of the Physic Garden, was a world devoted to gold. The herbs to cure the dropsy, or melancholy or the plague carried by the rats that come in up the river on the boats, lay under my windows in Chelsea; and if I could have learned their language I could perhaps have cured myself earlier of my own addiction to the base metal that was Dominic: but his transformations were too engaging, his alchemy too arresting, to make it possible for a time to walk back into – as I imagined – the dullness of everyday life. I was, for that time, a moll: in the Mayfair flat belonging to 'Aspers' – John Aspinall (before the initiation of gambling clubs and casinos, I see a vast table in the sitting-room, in-toxicating green baize, counters of a frosted pink and gold which would be handed out like sweets to girls who sat by the table's edge, and I hear, as in the most cliché-ridden movie, the clink of ice in glasses). —

Everything is transformed, here: money is frozen and solidified into oblong squares and marked casually with vast sums, quite plainly: £1,000 or more, no hieroglyphs in this ancient lingo and, such sums taken so lightly, fortunes are lost and won with a light elegance. Between the sip of scotch on the rocks and the slowing of the wheel or turning up of the unwelcome high card in *vingt-et-un*, Henry Vyner's Cistercian monastery Fountains Abbey and the surrounding Yorkshire forests turn to ash. Did Dominic think he could win, against the combined forces of James Goldsmith and the other millionaires who sit like buddhas in the artificial light, while the humdrum day pursues its unwanted patterns out-side? Did he see himself, husband of the heiress he thought I was, transmuting my family's riches into Rumpelstiltskin's gold? Certainly, his determination to win – to win a rich man's daughter, to win at cards and beat the world – brought the devil to our door; and one night, on returning late from his (rented? on approval?) Mayfair flat, it was to find the light on in the kitchen, my mother and father sitting in a state of anxiety at the table, with Agnes and John long upstairs asleep. An anonymous caller had announced my imminent end, the result of a motor crash 'in New Maldon' – and no amount of frantic phone calls had been able to locate me. I see my father's face, as he goes past me, past the tray of little yoghurt pots on the dresser where tomorrow's germ foments ready for another day of cleansing, of good health – and his heavy step on the stairs shows his grief and shock. He warns me not to go in fast cars: I feel the pain of seeing him confused. Heavier than Agnes, my father climbs the stairs and my mother says his heart is bad. Evil, in the shape of tabloid insinuations and more 'hoaxes', came to haunt us then.

The atlas of my world began to change. Regent's Park, Albany Street with its grey length, its one tobacconist and tiled, lavatorial White House at the Great Portland Street end, so hideous to my eye that I hurry past it when leaving the Underground there; the park, echoing in summer to the cries of Titania as Midsummer Night follows Midsummer Night, rain or shine in the open auditorium. Bedford College, with its secret 'Blue Garden' and beeches trained in a ball-dress hoop around the perimeter, Queen Mary's rose garden, formal so the tea roses seem ready for an Edwardian, cedar-lawned tea. The No. 3 and the No. 73, the buses that go from Albany Street, the bus stop just a matter of yards from Charlotte Havelka's front door, and carry her to Liberty's, to match up the buttons on the raspberry tweed or find the braid for the new fashion, curtains for my mother's room bordered in a rosy grosgrain ribbon. The streets of Mayfair, where my questionable life plays out: Mount Street and Curzon Street, Upper Grosvenor Street, for Dominic loves to walk up from Davies Street and flaunt himself in Claridges. The park – Hyde Park this time, with Park Lane a centre for the men my seducer jokingly calls 'gundogs' – or so I think he says at first, when we sit at the Duke of Wellington's end of Park Lane, late at night in the Milroy, the club from which the band for my dance was picked. The gundogs turn out to be a Greek pronunciation for contacts – contacts for deals, more deals, shady deals that fly up and down Park Lane. I am expected to produce gundogs myself: isn't my father an important man in the City? But I sit silent, as the band thumps and the rich Greeks talk over my head to the Apollo who will bring them into Society, with a nod of his fair crown. Then Swallow Street, this last of all in my night map: the Stork Room where Al Burnett cracks his jokes, whisky in teacups, a mushroom field of late gamblers laughing and shouting: 'I went to Monte Carlo to visit my money.' More laughter, more whisky and out into Regent Street, a neat circle formed before I go home. — I used to long for faraway places I had known when I bent over my atlas as a pupil at the school in St John's Wood that I went to before St Paul's, but soon I shall be tied to my spot, near my parents as ever and yearning to be the other side of the world, exploring, seeing, living on impulse – though the fatal results of such a life are visible in my family and my actions prove I fear adventure as much as I crave it. Chelsea is as far as I go: Royal Hospital Road, where the Chelsea Pensioners walk at a snail's pace in their gleam of scarlet and gold, the Royal Hospital itself, beautiful and austere, with its hidden pocket of glade and leafy path, Ranelagh Gardens, tucked away at the side, Flood Street, Cheyne Walk where the ghosts of Rossetti and Whistler and Turner walk down to Tite Street. (Colin buys Whistler's old house there and pulls it down, erecting an ugly modern white house in its place. More scandal, more obloquy. I watch it go up; I am invited in; a wrought-iron staircase, daintily carved in a marine design, replaces the old panelled rooms that looked out over the river to Battersea.) This Chelsea, where I move now in the year before I marry, is only just beginning to discover smartness and fashion. The King's Road has one new dress shop and a girl, immensely tall, half Scandinavian and with a mermaid's yellow hair, walks along it in the newest thing around, a sheepskin coat. Chelsea Manor Street, Old Church Street, Glebe Place, Markham Square. The circle forms in low-lying land that is not much changed since Walter Greaves's watercolours of little steamers going upriver, past Turner's studio where the street urchins taunted him and he was known as Puggy Booth.

From here, from our house in Swan Walk, the redbrick house in the little street of old houses that runs from Chelsea Embankment to Royal Hospital Road, I shall leave for my marriage on the 18th of November, just a month after my twentieth birthday. The last of the leaves on the trees in the grounds of the Royal Hospital are falling. The great black car comes now. Where is my suitcase? This limousine cannot contain anything so prosaic as luggage: has it been sent ahead to the Savoy, so I can change at the reception into my 'going away' outfit (the beige wool under the raspberry tweed) over which Charlotte has toiled all through summer and autumn in the mews of the house my father has now sold? Everything has been thought of. The car glides to the door of 6 Swan Walk and I get in, my father after me. We sit in silence in the great black car as I am ferried across the Styx in my dress of muted gold, back to the streets of Mayfair, to the Grosvenor Chapel in South Audley Street.

THREE

Doting

Henry Green

Born under Saturn, the planet of melancholy, the family I had married into is connected to mine by an infinitesimal number of rings, which, like those of the sinister ancient god, are icy, relics of a former whole. My grandmother Pamela, the daughter of Percy and Madeline Wyndham, represented the Bohemian side: Clouds, the house at East Knoyle where she grew up, was built by her parents to celebrate William Morris socialism and Burne-Jones, and had doubtless contributed to the 'unworldly' character she liked to display. Maud, my husband's grandmother, was from Petworth, and her father was Percy Wyndham's elder brother. Pamela had married my grandfather Eddy Tennant; Maud, a Yorke whose first name was Vincent and whose interests lay in an engineering business in Birmingham, London and Leeds. Pamela had been dead ten years by the time I was born; but Maud lived, at the time of my marriage; and it was to Bayswater, the place of shady squares and lodging-houses, the last resort of the unsuccessful girl in my family, my aunt Clare, that we went on the occasion of being invited to lunch with her.

The extreme old age of Maud and her housekeeper – both of whom shuffled into the hall of the old mansion block flat to greet us when we arrived – had obliterated any trace of the darkness that is the feature of this family. Her son Henry, my about-to-be father-in-law, had the look of a Spaniard, and other cousins showed the low hairline, the jet black hair and the handsome, saturnine appearance of those who can afford the luxury of melancholy. A yellow pigment in the skin, eyes as busy as coals just thrown on a fire, were all that remained, in Maud, of her family's 'otherness'. She was so old, bent and shrivelled, her head crowned by a few wisps of snow-white hair, that it was hard to believe her the mother of a genius so imbued with the sadness and absurdity of life that he had already, and still only in his fifties, withdrawn almost entirely from the world. Henry – who had taken the name Henry Green, to escape either the rings of his family or the duties of his father-dominated business, or maybe simply to declare himself an artist in these most daunting of circumstances; who knows – lived as far from Maud as it was possible, in those days, to be. It was from Trevor Place, from the small house where Henry and his wife – with a minuscule room for their son – lived in Knightsbridge, that we had gone 'North of the Park' to visit my husband's grandmother.

This part of the world, containing so many aunts and grandmothers on dwindling incomes, seemed already crepuscular and without hope by the time we were admitted at one o'clock to the great, gloomy flat. Shadows had collected in the hall by the table, itself as high as Maud. The housekeeper walked slowly and showed no pleasure at seeing us. In the murky dining-room we ate boiled meat and carrots and a pudding I forget; and, as if she had picked up my thoughts on the extreme slowness of the passing of time at this meal, Maud embarked on reminiscences of her childhood and youth at Petworth. The meals, she said, took so much time and contained so many courses that the ladies of the house brought their knitting in with them. As she spoke, I saw sadness behind the black eyes that burned in interest at meeting me, this latest loop in the family – a cousin brought in from her uncle's side – and I saw her mouth twisting to a smile as she spoke. Huntin', shootin' and knittin', said Maud Yorke, her thin gasp of laughter floating over the tiny coffee cups and the plodding shape of the maid, barely discernible in the gloom. I saw her for a moment, taller and straight, raven-haired as the rest of the family, smiling sardonically while game succeeds soup and roast meats the Petworth partridges and mallards and snipe, and pies and patties and creams and savouries are brought interminably in. Does Maud – as she tells me of her imprisoned youth at the table of her father, Lord Leconfield – feel envy for my grandmother, her bohemian cousin, Pamela? The children at Clouds, so my father had told me, famously ran free. Pamela's mother Madeline remained all her life a child, indoctrinated by her own mother's teaching of Rousseau; Maud's family, as perhaps she knew and fought against to no avail, was still of the old world, the *ancien régime*. But Maud Yorke, a minute later, speaks of the Hunt; and, as if in tribute, a shred of pink enters her cheeks and she turns to her grandson as she might to a young man at a hunt ball, a cackle audible now as the past comes galloping back: a stern dawn, white sky scudding over hedgerows, a muddy stream of barking, baying dogs. The melancholy strain in the family does not come from Maud: despite the aura of romantic rebellion I paint around her, my husband's grandmother, for all her tales of knitting her way through banquets, is not by nature a *tricoteuse*.

One evening in the autumn of 1957 I visited the house in Trevor Place where my future parents-in-law lived. Trevor Place leads from Trevor Square, with its small eighteenth-century houses and the imposing redbrick rear of Harrods store rooms; and to emerge into the Brompton Road from behind this building through the narrow passage provided is – or was, in those days when Knightsbridge was still a village as much inhabited by writers and those with small incomes as by bankers – a move from quietness and restraint into the impossible flamboyance of the Harrods façade. Windows dressed with luxurious and suddenly desirable items must daily have tempted my mother-in-law, as she crossed the wide thoroughfare and made for the more modest – and rare – provisioners of Knightsbridge. Time and again – on her way to change a book at the Harrods library on the third floor of the store (the librarian, Miss Clutton, was hard pressed to satisfy the twice-weekly habit of the Yorkes, and to supply satisfactory reading matter for Mr Yorke must have been especially hard: Adèle his wife might enjoy a light novel, but his tastes were changeable and surprising) – time and again, there must have been the temptation, on entering the portals of Harrods, to make for the famous Food Halls. The tables of shellfish, white biers laid with prawns, lobster and salmon, their age in death calculable from the glazed eye that looks out over banks of artificial moss, their prices upright on placards just above their heads, would have drawn this anxious housekeeper to spend unwisely. A crown of lamb, festive in white paper curlers for the dinner party ahead, would have appealed to this daughter of Herefordshire land-owners, from Ledbury where the red soil gapes under the grass. — She was born Adèle Biddulph but was known as Dig. — 'Henry and Dig!' said my aunt Clare to the world in general, standing in the drawing-room at Glen shortly after my engagement to their son was announced. 'They have so *little* money!'

Dig is standing in the hall of the house in Trevor Place. The hall has black-and-white squares on the floor, these, unusually, of carpet rather than lino or tiles: it is a touch of luxury in a house grown shabby over the years. She has an Edwardian face – and was, I believe, older than the brilliant, difficult man she had chosen to marry a quarter of a century before: her jaw is pronounced, eyes and nose well positioned and showing some of the consciousness of being or having once been a beauty; hair dyed a Venetian red piled in a frou-frou of curls with a comb, high on the head. In the Flemish perspective of black-and-white squares she looks out of place, uncertain, like a Dadaist joke. Her smile, showing a desire to please at all times, is reinforced by the embarrassment or irritation of the sound of heavy footsteps in the room above. Henry, as I am to come to understand, is walking to the drinks tray while his wife is out of the room. Tonight, we will go upstairs for half an hour or so. Dig will talk of Miss Clutton and the new Sansom novel too long borrowed by another user. Between the large, dominating portrait of Henry Green by Matthew Smith, which hangs to the right of the subject's wing chair, and my future father-in-law himself, is a gloom almost equal to that in the Bayswater flat of Henry's mother, Maud. The lamp, with its Thirties shade on the table beside him, appears to have had its light absorbed – by the yellowness of the portrait above, by the dark glower of the sitter in his chair. We go up and there is greeting; Henry's unexpected high-pitched laugh, again not unlike his mother's cackle, causes Dig to cast another rapid, apprehensive glance in my direction. The drinks tray, at the end of the narrow London L-shaped room, has barely an inch of gin remaining in a half-bottle of Gordon's. It is necessary to go out for more. The young man I will marry – their son, and, as I at first thought, almost a stranger to them after years away at school and at university – must go to the Grenadier Arms to buy another half. Henry subsides into his chair and begins to tease. 'Oh no, Henry,' Dig sighs. 'Gone too far?' Henry says, with a squeaking laugh. The half-bottle comes in. Later we will go to the Hotel Normandie for dinner, Henry wedged against a pink marble pillar with his black eyes staring impassively out at the empty tables and few diners.

All summer – a summer which saw the refusal of the young man I was to marry to sit the Oxford exams for which he was tipped to gain a First – I had found myself under the spell of Henry. Whether he saw me any differently from the girls he loved and laughed at in his novels I don't know; I knew his sentences, in *Doting*, where the young girl's legs 'start from her knickers' and in *Loving*, where Charley Raunce the butler lies in bed as the bells ring, with 'cunty fingers' after a night with an Irish maid; and I could tell, from the expression of profound cynicism and frequent retelling of anecdotes too obscure to be risqué but certainly intended to fill the category 'Gone Too Far', that I counted, for him, as a girl.

I saw no future, it is true, as anything else. Henry's son, with his handsome, melancholy face, head larger proportionately than his body – this comparative smallness accounted for, he told me, by having been given gin to drink by his father as a child – seemed as little prepared for the marriage suddenly thrust upon him as myself. Steeped in gloom, he confided to me in a nightclub that his most compelling desire was to find himself in a crashing sports car, travelling at a great speed. — Yet it was for this hereditary sadness and lack of wish to belong to the world that I liked him: the son of Henry Yorke – their descent was from the family of the Earls of Hardwicke – had, on being called to National Service, refused a commission. Potatoes were handed round in the officers' mess by this young private. — Again, I don't know whether Henry's influence was at work here, whether the author of an accurate depiction of working life (in Birmingham, the setting for his novel *Living*, which shows the Works belonging to Henry's much-feared and hated father Vincent Yorke) had much to do with his only son's decision to eschew the privileges of his class. It seems likely that Henry's ear for dialogue and his empathy with the men who worked for Pontifex – such was and is to this day the name of the family engineering business – would have affected the silent young man to whom I found myself on that November afternoon related both by blood and by impending marriage. Father and son liked to wear suits of a dark grey cloth, these bearing the marks of much wear and an evident antipathy to dry cleaning. It was clear to any observer that Dig, despite her insistence on the 'allrightness' of things (this conveyed by the sweetest and most constant of smiles, and a great deal of delighted laughter as if accompanying her unusual family to a flower show or any other harmless and 'pretty' occasion), found the shabbiness and sheer dirtiness of her husband and son hard to countenance. If, for a girl, it was hard to understand what tie bound the romantic, lecherous and frequently ash- and drink-stained Henry with this most conventional and harassed of women, it was necessary for an answer to look to the past. 'Why!' Henry exclaims as we sit too long over cold, unpalatable coffee in the Hotel Normandie, and the recent return from honeymoon by separate routes of a young couple is discussed, 'we would never have done that! We clung together like birds . . .'

Henry and Dig now are an odd pair of birds, and Henry's visitors do not encourage in him the cleanliness poor Dig would like. I see, in that summer, before the announcement by Henry Green that he has 'Spanish royalties – dinars, is it?'– followed by a cackle – 'can't spend them here apparently, might as well go there' – before our improbable visit to Spain – the round of evenings in Trevor Place. There was the pull between Dig's need for dinner parties and a 'proper' life (a Spanish servant lived in the basement, a lift came up electrically into the floor above like a jack-in-the-box, bearing meals which Henry inevitably refused), and the almost nightly drinking caller, most often Arthur Koestler. The little squares of Aubusson carpet, cut down, like Dig's expectations, from a grander, more ordered pattern, rucked under Koestler's and Henry's feet as they sat opposite each other in the doll's house in Trevor Place. From time to time, inebriated beyond their stomachs' endurance, philosopher and writer would be sick, the Aubusson squares receiving the brunt of it. — None of this, as I heard about it at the time, reduced my infatuation with my future father-in-law's strange quality – which was, I suppose, the quality of writing itself of genius – and I welcomed the trip to Spain, to (as Henry put it with a lugubrious shake of the head) 'the Costa Brava!', without giving a thought to the problems, both organisational and culinary, that would be bound to arise for Dig.

From an upper window in the house in Trevor Place – a house, bizarrely, left almost immediately after their son's marriage and exchanged for a taller and more spacious house in Wilton Place, the lack of a child to accommodate somehow underlined by the move – Henry liked to remark that he could see 'Violet, as she goes to bed' in her house No. 1 Trevor Square. 'Oh duck – you can't really,' comes his wife's protest: we are sitting, as so often before, in the first-floor drawing-room with its air, both arranged and suggestive, of a temporary domicile (we all look uncertain here, it is a room for 'grand' people to sit in but an abundance of books combined with Henry's atmosphere, cigarette smoke, glasses with flat gin and tonic and no hint of lemon, and the brooding yellowness of the Matthew Smith portrait, make it seem like a theatrical set). Henry is well advanced in his teasing. He has several times already Gone Too Far, and we await his remarks on his elder brother Gerald, with whom we are invited to stay – all this before the trip to Spain will take place. But Henry, from his deep chair where the shadows he engenders have gathered round his dark face, black brows and mouth that is both generous and cruel, likes only to talk of his spying. — Years later, I find in his memoir *Pack My Bag*:

> In one house which overlooked another a boy could see into a maid's room across the way and she did not draw the blinds when she undressed. Night after night long after he should have been in bed he sat up till half-past ten and every night she went to bed, of course, taking off her clothes to do it. Their windows were some way apart, there was almost nothing he could make out except the glint of flesh, but it worked on him to this extent that he had to go away for the whole of one term to rest. And yet, if he had been closer, if she had undressed in his room, he would almost certainly have been appalled. He may have realised this because he never tried to get to know her

– and I wonder if that boy, in Henry's early life, had given him a taste for looking out of windows at another who does not know they are watched; along with a desire not to know, but to keep a distance from people: to write or fall in love (famously, his entry in *Who's Who* has as his hobby 'romancing over a bottle of wine'); certainly, to be with Henry is to feel that for one to get closer would make him appalled.

Violet, whom Henry claims to spy on while Dig laughs as she always laughs, as if a farce is being acted out in this unsettling room, is in fact the widow of my grandmother Pamela's younger brother, Guy Wyndham. I already know her as the kindest and funniest of women and I shrink from Henry's high-pitched cackle and Dig with her 'Duck, you don't, you *know* you don't' — and, not for the first time, I wish myself elsewhere. I am marrying a ghost, the ghost of poetry – for in the young man to whom I am engaged I see only his father: in all his rumpled, ash-bestrewn state, drunk and frequently filled with bile, Henry Green will inspire me – so I must have believed, for, like so many, I knew I must one day write. The talk turns from the upper lavatory and its secret view and we rise, I knowing as I leave that I shall be teased when I have gone; that the Tennants are considered rich and vulgar, that the existence of John McCubbin and Agnes and the dinner parties in the house in Chelsea fill Henry with contempt. He half rises, to say goodbye. — 'Going to Forthampton this weekend?' he is finally unable to resist saying; and as I turn, startled, I see (as in a horror movie, where the 'good' wife tries to turn the victim away from her fate) Dig shaking her head and beginning her refrain – 'Oh duck, *please don't,*' as Henry wags his finger in an ogrish way, enjoying his enactment of a sinister pantomime. 'Mad. Quite mad.' He rolls his eyes. 'Sold his soul to Satan.' He turns to his son, and then his wife. 'Watch out, at Forthampton!' The witch's laugh follows us down the stairs. — Dig runs down, to stand on the black-and-white carpeted squares, the gracious hostess kissing my cheek and bidding us goodnight.

I would find it hard to say which of the two visits made to or with the Yorkes in the summer of that year prior to my wedding was the most disturbing. Forthampton Court, the childhood home of Henry and his elder brother Gerald, is near Tewkesbury in Gloucestershire; it dates, as guidebooks would say, to Tudor times and earlier, and would have remained an interesting edifice with historical associations and within sound of the Tewkesbury Bells if it had not been for the elder son Gerald's decision, at an early age, to devote himself to mysticism and the arcane works of Tibetan monks. This interest was followed by an allegiance with Aleister Crowley, progenitor of the Beast and 666 and all manner of Satanic stuff: Gerald was cut off by his father from any chance of inheritance as a result; and Henry, who probably enjoyed this unusual twist in the fortunes of a family as conventional as a businessman, Vincent, and his wife Maud could make it, liked to play out the role of astonished onlooker, tourist at evil's shrine. — We had been warned there would be a pentacle chalked in a corner of the Great Hall when we arrived, and so there was. Gerald and his wife bustled forward to meet us, the wife apparently playing no part in the summoning into the five-sided diagram of an Indian familiar who was, like a *spécialité de la maison*, promised for this evening's fare. We sat at a long trestle table; there was talk of children born with supernumerary nipples, as I remember, and an air of impatience on the part of Gerald (he was taller and more gaunt than his brother) at the failure of the Indian visitor to arrive. She or he came, however, just as we finished coffee, some message was spelt out; then, despite the excitement and subsequent satisfaction of the host at this phenomenon, we were informed briskly that it was time for bed. Up the stairs, a different set of stairs from that of Gerald's nephew, the young man I was to marry, I was dispatched. The room was small and felt to me haunted: a dark mahogany cupboard, gigantic in my wakeful but dozing state, dominated my anxious dreams. — What was it that held this scholarly, even brilliant man in the thrall of Crowley? Was this translator of ancient texts from the Tibetan – manuscripts arrived in the Gloucestershire post at breakfast as we sat at the table by the side of a burnt-out fire and a half-rubbed-out pentacle – in fact 'mad', as Henry, with much gloating, liked to pretend? Henry and Gerald, who appeared to be as unlike each other as it was possible to be, were nevertheless more alike than they believed. They possessed some quality which, like the invisible visitor in the Great Hall at Forthampton, delivered information from another sphere. — It is hard to resist coming to this conclusion.

Henry wrote of his first perceptions of girls: 'the lightness I did not know the weight of, the different way they moved and literally then it seemed as though they were walking in water over their heads along the glaring street . . .' And I must have felt I walked under water in Spain, for I was a girl literally out of my depth, in the presence of Henry Green and his wife and the American writer Terry Southern. The extent of my girlitude was clear, from the moment we arrived, at the depressing villa near Barcelona rented by Henry's publishers in order for him to enjoy his royalties (I think his Spanish publisher did come to see him once, but I was too entranced, too fascinated by the daily and nightly scene in the loggia, where Henry and the scabrous writer of *Candy* talked and drank deep into the night, to take him – or anyone else – in). Like the lizard which lay long hours without a twist or turn and then with a flick was gone as if cut from the rough white wall with a paperknife, I sat noticed and unnoticed in a wicker chair, eyes trained on the genius of Henry. Southern, who was to commemorate the meeting in a famous interview in *Paris Review* – Henry feigned an even greater deafness than that from which he already suffered and when asked if some aspect of his work was subtle, replied that he had no anticipation of his wife, at his death, performing suttee – chuckled into glass after glass of Fundador. His wife Carol – according to Henry she slept 'right at the bottom of the bed' – must have helped Dig in the kitchen, which was as unappetising and depressing as the rest of the villa. I was not even a girl who helped. In some way I thought myself invisible, drinking in the at times malevolent magic of a writer to whom words appeared to descend, like the visitations of the angels in Florentine paintings, straight from the sky above on to his head. I was giddy, in the underwater atmosphere of this charmless place, where Henry, never leaving his chair and drink in the loggia, would point delightedly out at the view. 'First, the cars' – we

were indeed positioned on a main road and it only
came to me many years later that the way of life
chosen by her husband must have been painful for
Dig to bear. For they had married in the Twenties
and enjoyed the life of Bright Young Things for a
decade, before Henry turned away from smartness to
the pub, the armchair in his London sitting-room, the
infrequent meetings at the London office of the
family firm. How much more elegant and beautiful
for her their trip abroad would have been before this
writer of proletarian lives and upper-class sillinesses
had decided to abandon society life! 'Then the trains,'
Henry goes inexorably on, looking at me (I think) in
the dank loggia before looking up, as in his cups he
often does, to check the position of the gecko.
'Beyond the railway —' Henry shakes his head in
mock despair and gloom. 'The turds in the sea —'
and he makes a gesture of a fleet of slowly moving
faeces: there is no reason to suppose him wrong. —
But I know, when he speaks of Spenser or Herrick or
Austen, how he loves their words. And I can sense
that Henry loves this mournful holiday – although of
course none of this is kind to Dig.

Dig, despite her formal manners and the conventional atmosphere (her hair, even in this undemand-
ing setting, is each day combed and curled and piled
high; pearls are placed round the neck like relics of a
long-dead religion and the table in the dark, bad-
smelling dining-room is laid, to the bafflement of the
local Spanish girl, as if an Edwardian dinner will
shortly be in full swing) – Dig retains her own essence
of a girl, and an independent girl at that. Henry may
be clever, gifted and scornful: Dig does not waver

from expressing her thoughts and opinions; and I come to see there is love still between this unusual couple and that, if anyone is left out of this odd happiness it is probably their son. How do Henry and Dig communicate? Too interested in my attempt to capture the seeds of inspiration and creation which to my besotted eye fly about the head of the unmoving man in the corner of the loggia, it never occurs to me to try and find out. — Henry's stories, of vile accidents with dentists, of a woman miscarrying in the latest model of bath on show at Earls Court manufactured by Vincent's firm (this anecdote causing loud laughter from Terry – future writer of *Strangelove* and already no stranger to the macabre or plain disgusting) – all the repertoire comes out as we sit in this ugly, built-over stretch of the Costa Brava and watch the effluvia of modern life wash by. Dig laughs, or laughingly protests: I see her only in that villa in our subaqueous meetings in dark hallways and passages. A mirror makes us four, doubles her sweet but stubborn smile – then I fall into my room and pull down a chipped blind, to escape the domination of the sun.

FOUR

Blues in the Night

Sebastian Yorke and Emma Tennant,
Grosvenor Chapel, 1957

I am sitting on the kitchen table in my parents' house in Swan Walk. My legs are swinging; I have regressed from girl – my engagement has returned me with a sense of sharp relief to the state I occupied before my abduction to the Underworld, the cries of Banco! and the roll of the dice – to something approximating a ten-year-old child. My mother looks at me guardedly. We are in the kitchen because it is Agnes and John's night out and therefore a Saturday: we will heat Agnes's soup with its glistening hat of grease and afterwards eat something cold, with a salad we make ourselves (I am as useless as anyone who never enters a kitchen at this simple task: later, my father will look down in silent surprise at the still-wet lettuce, the badly chopped tomato, the dressing which lacks the mustard and sugar he likes to include). We are in the kitchen for another reason also. The young man I will marry is one floor up, in the sitting-room where my parents have built a wide window that overlooks the Chelsea Physic Garden and the river. He will not face this spectacular view of the Thames and the then trackless unknown of Battersea on the far shore. He faces my father, on the side of the room that has the elegant fireplace jutting out, the china deer (I don't know where the Meissen birds have gone: perhaps they were part of the entail from father to son and have been sold by my elder half-brother already) and the low tables with their bunches of autumn cycla-men. There is nowhere in the room where documents or papers could be laid out – there isn't a study in the whole house, which is smaller than 13 Chester Terrace and must yet contain me (at the top, ripe cherries on the wallpaper, an attic next door through which a burglar has crept, now bolted by John), my sister Catherine and, with as formal a pretence of their separate sleeping habits as a grand country house before the war, a room each for Agnes and John McCubbin. My about-to-be fiancé and my father must shuffle evidence of their preparedness to protect and provide for me, on their knees: papers showing the state of Henry's firm (bad: my father will suggest an adviser and the young man who discusses the finance of proposing to this daughter of a rich cousin will accept the offer in due course); and lists, the lists my father loved to make, of all the possible items of expenditure in our future life together. I must live, of course, and my putative husband and I will share the cost (£4,000 for a twenty-one-year lease) of a maisonette, also overlooking the river, in Cheyne Walk and not more than three minutes' walk away. The rent is £7 a week. I shall continue my girl-hood there, undisturbed by the demands of matrimony: already I buy the china and cutlery I am accustomed to at my parents' house and sit with my mother choosing fabrics for curtains and carpets which exactly echo hers. Like an infant monkey sep-arated too soon from maternal care, I cling to shreds: of good taste; of materials and colours like the com-fort blankets needed by babies. Yet even with this security ahead, I feel a deep ache of uncertainty as I swing my legs against the sides of the kitchen table and my mother goes calmly and slowly about the preparation of the salad. The announcement of the engagement goes in *The Times* tomorrow. I think of the temporary flat in Oakley Street where we will live while the upper maisonette at 8 Cheyne Walk is painted and refurbished to resemble my old home – and of its owner, Isobel Strachey. Isobel, the most absent-minded and indecisive of women, had nevertheless, in a fit of impatience with an admirer, placed an announcement of her betrothal to him, also in *The Times* – and had subsequently been forced to countermand it. I felt for her humiliation but couldn't help admiring the independence of spirit which had led to her putting it there in the first place. I am concealing a longing (as I was even then dimly aware) to cancel the four stiff lines of my engagement to Sebastian, the son of Mr Henry and the Honourable Mrs Yorke, and run off into the sunset. I am also aware that the young man who seals the agreement with my father upstairs probably feels the same.

My mother prepares coffee for the end of the dinner which lies ahead. My fiancé will go back to the L-shaped room, the gin and the crashes and groans from the basement which precede the dinner hour. We in turn will act out a semblance of a 'normal' evening; but without John there are endless trips to be made back to the kitchen – forgotten pepper and salt; wine glasses; a butter knife and so on. My father sits absolutely still as my mother and I play out the pretence that Agnes is really here: that dinner is the same as all other dinners on other nights of the week, with John standing directly behind my father's chair and in front of the sideboard, his features stern and only the occasional wild burst of laughter, quickly smothered.

On these occasions my father sometimes spoke of the family business and as he addressed me I thought only of the names he let drop – of companies, of ventures and partnerships – and I allowed my mind to wander. In this room where every picture, and even the dark mahogany table and the dining chairs were fruits of endeavour, grasp and a merging of interest and capital, I found it hard to make the link, so heavily had it been concealed, between the words and money, profit and loss. I knew my father's aunt, Margot, had declared her lack of interest in money, which was 'no more than almonds and raisins' to her; and I think now she must have whiled away the time playing with words as her father expounded on the industry which had brought her a house in Cavendish Square, a wardrobe of dresses by Worth, and a Prime Minister for a husband. For Margot, unconsciously perhaps, had been thinking of currency, when she threw out the brave statement about almonds and raisins – a 'currantcy' which indeed occupied her all her days, as she was constantly begging Sir Charles for more. — The Mysore Gold Mining Company; The United Alkali Company; Coromandel Gold Mines of India; Tharsis Sulphur and Copper Company; Nobel Dynamite Trust; The Steel Company of Scotland; North British Railway; Assam Railways and Trading Company; British South African Explosives; Chicago Great Western Railway: these were some of Sir Charles's chairmanships and, in the case of New York, Pennsylvania and Ohio Railroad Co. and the aforementioned Chicago Great Western, he was a member of their finance committee or a voting trustee from London. It was impossible to hear this litany of

romance and greed without imagining myself once
more in my room at Glen, the Doocot, where a
strange picture by an obscure artist above the fireplace
depicted a train rushing across a drear but terrifying
landscape. As I had also, at that stage in my life,
played over and over again the few records to be
found by the side of the cupboard-sized radiogram in
the Glen drawing-room – and in particular the haunting song with the words 'A woman's a two-face, a
worrisome thing who'll leave ya to sing the blues in
the night' – this warning followed by the hoot of a
train as it crosses the wide prairie – '*Hear* dat lone-
some whistle blowin' cross the trestle, Whooee' – I
would dream of night trains, of desertion and longing,
while my father outlined the exports of C. Tennant
Sons. The tiger-striped Mysore Mines in India – this
at least was how I saw the place which, according to
my father, had been 'found' by the unusual method
(this Sir Charles again) of throwing his gold pince-nez
on a map of India and commanding that excavations
should proceed immediately there – also took me far
on imaginary journeys as we ate.

The invention of bleach, or, more accurately,
chlorine liquor, which had been the mainspring of the
family fortune, interested me less, however often I
might be reminded in books around the house of the
revolution in bleaching of linen and cotton previously
left out to receive the wan rays of a Scottish sun and
then, as a result of the scientific brilliance of my great-
great-great-grandfather, whitened overnight by the
application of bleach. Early photographs of the great
chimney, Tennant's Stalk in Glasgow, godfather of
pollution and besmircher of the landscape for miles

around, were also less than engaging; but my father, who never pushed these memorabilia of the early days of the Industrial Revolution at me, only smiled when I fidgeted and changed the subject if the Works, St Rollox in Glasgow, came up. He thought me like his mother Pamela, perhaps, who had refused to look out of the window of the train on approaching Waverley Station in Edinburgh, for fear of seeing C. TENNANT blazoned on the hoardings there. — Or he simply thought me a girl. I was, as I have said, more like a child – as possibly he saw on this evening just prior to my marriage. I enjoy hearing of the gold piece of eight which my father describes again – he will fetch it later – that came from 'a branch of Tennants 1,000 miles up the Amazon'. This time he will give it to me. The cruel Spanish profile on the gold coin goes in my mind down on a wooden counter – but I have no idea, of course, of what it bought. A picture of this 'branch of Tennants' – a trading-post presumably, surrounded by the atrocities of conquest – becomes as firmly engraved on my mind as are the features of the *Treasure Island* pirate on the metal I now hold in my hand – and I see, as my fingers close round it, the afternoon sun and deep shadow in the tiny store, all images from the then hugely successful *Outcast of the Islands* of Carol Reed. — I sense the restlessness, of capture and discovery, in the piece of eight in my grasp, and I know the need to travel, explore, stride across the world like a man. My father talks of his recent trip to the Tharsis Mine in Spain (some of those far-flung chairmanships are his now, passed down from his grandfather) and he describes the little train which took him from the summit down into the mine where copper and sulphur are produced. — I smell the bad-egg smell of sulphur and ask to hear more of the West Indian property, with, it is said, a great lake of black pitch, which had been Sir Charles's too. But my father does not care for the West Indies. An estate rots gently in Trinidad, unvisited by him since an early trip brought jaundice and a hatred of the place. — I feel I shall never go there. My father is ruler of his demesnes, whether long ago sold or disposed of, or of the present day, and the man I am about to marry has not so much as a Coromandel or a Mysore to his name. I try to think of him and of my visits to him in Oxford, where we spent long, cold days, armed only by the arrival of a coffee bar – the first espresso to reach these shores, so black and repelling at first, so strong and finally so addictive. As we sit over pasta (again, there's not much of this in the England of the time) the proprietor of the bar (named the Cantina) comes up to us and bows and smiles. His name is Esposito. My father, to help an indigent relative, invested in the espresso bar: the young man I wish to marry and I will always be given a table, despite a queue of hungry students. Cold roast beef, more pasta, cup after minuscule cup of coffee. — Wherever I go, however far – or so I felt then – the tentacles of the family are there.

If my father sits on by his empty coffee cup – of 'mocha' brown china, glazed, with a white interior where the remains of coffee sugar, another new addition to the luxuries contrived or imported since the end of the war, glitters like black diamonds at the base – then I return to him when my mother and I have washed up. We are still in our pretence that there is nothing out of the usual on this Saturday night, despite the absence of Agnes and John – and the unmentioned recent conversation conducted by my father and Sebastian on the subject of money. I will not think of the wedding ceremony ahead, nor of the gold dress, its choice of cloth both ostentatious and muted, as if to demonstrate that entry into so profoundly disaffected and melancholy a family as Henry Green's can be marked only by a muffled bell, a gold dulled almost to worthlessness. My mother will certainly not calculate the seating in the chapel – with a wedding of people who are related, and with the additional fact that a number of my mother's writer and artist friends are also allies of the parents of the groom, this will in the event be hard to do. Instead she will put her head to one side as a key scrapes in the lock of the door in the hall; while my father, either talking or in profound silence, sits over his reflection in the polished mahogany of the table, the pink dome of his head rising like an Eastern sun to the side of an abandoned fruit plate.

I cannot say if I remember when I was told the details of the joint income – £2,000 a year – on which my husband and I would live, but I can be certain it was not on that quiet, unremarkable evening in the autumn of 1957, when Agnes and John, back early from a visit to the pictures in the King's Road or Fulham Road, let themselves into the house and went into the kitchen. I could imagine Agnes's brief inspection of the draining-board and wire basket containing plates and cutlery, alien objects when not washed up by her hands: I hear her sniff and mutter something in her strong Czech accent. — My mother indicates we should all go upstairs and we do. But something – in the memory of espresso coffee which our own tame filter type inspires perhaps, or in my own impending departure from this family home to which we have so recently moved from Regent's Park – makes me feel there is change ahead. Upstairs, as if the subject must emerge somehow, the approaching wedding is briefly discussed. I insist there shall be a minimum of guests. What do I try to hide? — a desire for a ceremony that will announce re-initiation into girlhood, Eleusinian rites to restore a lost virginity? It is impossible to say. — But it is agreed, without controversy, that such friends of my mother's as Stephen and Natasha Spender, Cyril Connolly, Martin and 'Pinkie' Beckett and 'Pom' and Lionel Brett, shall be invited solely to the reception at the Savoy Hotel. My father, who does not admit to friends as it is considered his role to assume the burden of the family, closes his eyes on the sofa: it is not for him to seat Violet Wyndham, his uncle's widow, or his sister Clare or – in the unlikely event he is prepared to leave Wilsford – his brother Stephen. We have concluded that the marriage rites will take place before a limited congregation.

There is almost no doubt that Henry (who will of course claim to have no feelings on the subject) and Dig will concur. Dig's Biddulph relatives will also be invited only to the Savoy Hotel – and, as it happens, will come with golden Labradors and a greater interest in the canine world than in bride or groom. Dig's sister, Mary Curry, will surely be invited to the chapel. Whether my half-brother Colin and his wife, and his younger brother James, with Emily Fawaz, recently married, will attend I do not know; there is no possibility of discussing this with my father, on his weekend evening away from the cares of the office. — Besides this, an increased tension in the air of past weeks suggests 'Nobody Knows the Trouble I Seen': whether it be David, demanding financial advice on his own remarriage, trouble with the aforementioned James, who writes to his father periodically on the subject of a gold half-sovereign he claims was lost in the kitchen garden at Glen, this showing for some reason a preference on the part of his father for the elder brother. Or, as I remember, the dramatic appearance on the doorstep in streaming rain of a young woman, one of the family, seeking sanctuary from a violent husband. — I remember her words: 'Christopher –' (to my father) – 'what do you think I am worth on the open market?' — All this was enough for my father to deal with; and may even have been one of the reasons for my choice of a quiet, smooth wedding – though, as it happened, there was no such thing as a quiet and uneventful occasion in our family.

The change I foresaw that evening turned out to involve Agnes and John as well as myself, officially to depart the portals of 6 Swan Walk and be handed over to Henry's son at the end of a short aisle in South Audley Street. Agnes and Charlotte and John (who had shared more than the life of Chester Terrace: they had once travelled to Czechoslovakia together, a journey apparently fraught with perils, for John McCubbin, in an attempt to gather wild flowers on the border, was shot at by guards and was fortunate to escape) were, as I had assumed from my earliest childhood, inseparable. When I was sent north at the outbreak of war, Agnes came – and John, when he could be spared in London by my father, could be seen on the lawn behind the house, playing with a young child, either myself or my brother, before re-entering the basement at the summons of the short-tempered Agnes. With the new wind that blew through the country – a wind bringing the scent of espresso coffee – came a woman who would replace Agnes. In a year or two, Luisa will walk around the kitchen downstairs, slamming pots down on the stove. Luisa is Italian.

This rift, consisting of the retirement of Agnes and the entrapment and subsequent scorn of Luisa for John McCubbin, lies in the future at the time of the picture in the *Daily Express*, of 19th November, shown here, of my exit, with husband, from the Grosvenor Chapel. At the time, Agnes Kabicek, John McCubbin and Charlotte Havelka are as much a part of the 'do-without wedding of the year' (as the *Express* billed it, exclaiming at the lack of a wedding cake) as Henry and Dig's family or mine. They stand in the great first floor reception rooms of the Savoy, looking out at the river as it flows fast down to Swan Walk and on to the sea, and John is laughing, bent double as always at the story a friend from Scotland, Tommy, tells of John's fire-engine tactics when driving the old Wolseley at Glen on the way to meet my father off the train at Galashiels station. I think to myself, as I walk over ('the bride was dressed in gold lamé') that I prefer their company to the '300 guests drinking champagne' and I laugh too at Tommy's story, a story I know well, of John's dash across the rabbit trap in the drive, the consequent wrenching off by a post too narrowly shaved of the door handle on the passenger side, and my father's surprised reaction to the state of the car. 'Rotten!' John and Tommy both sway and bend with laughter again, at the reason given for the sudden dereliction of the Wolseley. 'Rotten!' — The laughter ceases when I go to the upstairs room at the Savoy and don Charlotte's trousseau. — I come down the stairs. — I am joined by the groom; all at once, as if a curtain had come down on the staged merriment, I am excluded from the party and the fun and driven in another long black car to another hotel, the Ritz, where a room and a sitting-room without flowers gloomily await us. — But what did I expect? We are young but not disposed to be cheerful. The blight – for the lack of which I believe I saw my parents thanking their good fortune at the ceremony and later at the reception – arrives in the form of the newspapers next day. 'Dominic Elwes Elopes With Heiress' – he has chosen, to the minute, the time of his revenge.

We go to Paris, then to Rome and thence to the King George Hotel in Beirut. When we return, and open the door into the thin, scruffy hall at 52 Oakley Street, it is to find a true impediment to our marriage. An enormous refrigerator blocks the passageway. We are just able to edge past, leaving our luggage by the front door. On the side of the fridge is pasted a card wishing us many congratulations from C. Tennant Sons. My father cannot have organised this; his assistant Arthur probably has. I feel the breath of ice all night, as I lie in the front ground floor bedroom that looks out on the bus stop.

FIVE

The Vice Bar

Judy's shoes
(by Antonia Fraser)

'Memories lie slumbering within us for months and years, quietly proliferating, until they are woken by some trifle and in some strange way blind us to life.' Chateaubriand, in his *Mémoires d'outre-tombe*, summoning Proust's madeleine over a century before the famous biscuit transported Marcel back into the past; and in the case of Judy's shoes a mention by a friend, Antonia, that she is possessor of a photograph of a pair of these – smart and feminine, giving a misleading impression of the wearer – takes me to Rome; to an ancient island in the Tiber: to the vaulted, whitewashed rooms and dark-smelling kitchen where Judy lived.

Judy Montagu is tall – though not as tall as I am, by the time I have shed the gold lamé dress and bridal outfit, put myself in high red heels and set out in my quest to escape the realities of life as a young married in Chelsea in 1960. I tower over Judy, yet her imperious manner, beak nose, sparse hair which gives the appearance of a balding cockatoo and her brandished cigarette (STOP the name of the Italian brand; indeed the powerful poison which can be felt going into the lungs should encourage obedience to the name) give an impression of great height. Of any age – she must in fact have been about thirty-eight – and of apparent disregard of her sex (no visit to the hairdresser, no amount of panicky grooming before a smart luncheon party could give a *soignée* air of femininity to this Roman Emperor, recently taken up residence on the Tiber's banks), Judy is as careful of her reputation as wit and gossipmonger as she appears careless of her looks. Roman High Society flocks to the disused morgue where she drinks whisky, flicks ash into the brown swirling river and destroys those who dare to cross her. I am here, a guest and possibly a protégée of Judy, because of her great friendship with my half-brother Colin. As a result of this and the regular visits from Princess Margaret to a place considered dangerously bohemian – the Isola Tiberina is in Trastevere, a quarter considered as insalubrious as, say, Soho would have been for a member of the sanitised post-war era Royal Family to be seen dead in – the Colonnas and the Buoncompagnias and the de Robillants and the Volpis come in large numbers. Invitations for 'the Brute', as her English friends term her, pour in. Judy knits and cross-pollinates the scandals, murders, suicides and simple seaside picnics of these families and at night, when she 'yobs through' (her term for discussion, for the summing-up of the day's tragedies and comic disasters), the whisky and the STOP make a kind of terrestrial halo around her. — The river sleeps beyond the long windows with their accompanying hooks where corpses latterly hung before burial. Adriana the maid (who will steal the stiff jewellery Dig gave me, the Cartier rubies set Indian-style on gold bangles) will not come in till morning. No one knows why their possessions disappear yet: Judy's haze is too enveloping; and it is dangerous to lose her latest pronouncement or look beyond the next party, in palazzo, villa or club. Nicknames, private words and phrases make up her world of the living as it is dissected and lovingly rearranged in this vaulted store-room of the dead in the Isola Tiberina. (Antonioni has used the room with its watery view and low vaulted ceiling, its air of slightly sordid mystery, in his film *L'Avventura* but there is no sense, while Judy is occupant, of the enigma of his characters.) Judy is downright; jokes are the currency; and the folly of human nature, of aspirations and disappointments, is the stuff of her talk. Her shoes, as the evening nears its end, are kicked off. I see them next day as they are placed by Adriana, side by side, awaiting Judy's late awakening. — For after all the talk and the whisky and STOP, Judy needs to sleep till well past midday. Her little room on the first floor of the Piazza San Bartolemmeo looks out on the old stone bridge with its head of Janus, the two-faced god, and, despite the fragility and age of the little road over the bridge, the cars and taxis that make their way to the old hospital, the only other building on the island apart from the morgue.

While Judy sleeps in this mirrorless house in the middle of the Tiber, those girls who are her guests – she has many, they are another draw to the young nobility of Rome: open in manner, as well as morals, they must seem, after the Italian princesses and heiresses, too good to be true – wander warily on the tiled floors upstairs or plague Adri as she makes coffee in a kitchen hung vertiginously over water. There is no question of going out without Judy: we sit on hard beds in barely furnished downstairs bed-rooms which smell of rotting brickwork. I try to read the *Guide bleu*; to learn of the remains of a Roman temple to Aesculapius that is buried on this tiny island; but my head is giddy; I am already feeling the effects of my foolish whisky and tap water, taken on arrival some days before. — I know Aesculapius to have been the god of healing; and that the ill and mad were carried to the temple, to sleep and thus to dream away their illness – but I don't know yet how badly I will need that sanctuary, lost now under the later additions and accretions of this Roman palimpsest.

Judy calls down for Adri; the day has begun. Her dresses I remember as mainly brown, as if autumn had settled on this brilliant spinster (who will nevertheless marry, and soon); and her shoes, as high and pointed as her dresses are shapeless and baggy are not far removed from the Italian chic of (say) her friend Laetizia Buoncompagnia, known by Judy as 'Tits Goodcompany'. The first Bloody Mary goes down; shall we leave for the Vice Bar in the Via Condotti? – or eat al fresco at a club, or send Adri out to the markets of Trastevere to fetch food for lunch here? We will go to the Vice Bar – we always do – tiny with not even a stool to sit on, vodka as Bullshots, vodka as Bloodys, white truffles in the long bread sandwiches, gossip humming along with an espresso machine that is sleeker and larger by far than anything in Oxford or my newly deserted King's Road. Where do we all meet tonight? Ruffo Ruffo – such indeed is his name – will come in his bright red sports car to take Kate or Liz out to dinner and on to the 84, the Ottanto Quattro, where the dancing goes on until after even Judy has gone to sleep in her room that is an annexe to the room of the dead on the Isola Tiberina. 'Chéri, je t'aime, chéri je t'adore, come la salsa di pomodoro' – the song has caught up Judy's 'girls' and we dance, oblivious to shame, responsibility or any of the puritan virtues instilled in our northern backgrounds. We *are* Italy; we are loved as much as the scarlet overcoat of all Italian food, tomato sauce.

I have no more idea of responsibility at this time than I had as a child, when John would cover up for my mistakes and May, seeing my lack of desire to take the blame for things that were patently my fault, shook her head and burrowed in the box of 100 Players before pretending to search deep in a bag for a match. I am, by the time I'm visiting Judy every two months or so, the mother of a child, a son whom I love and take along Royal Hospital Road to Ranelagh Gardens in his pram. I have passed my twenty-first birthday (eight months pregnant I sat with my mother in her house and wore a hat of ostrich feathers made by Simone Mirman, which must have looked strange atop my huge girth: was I always frivolous? – or simply trying to banish the blue devil, as the poet Fitzgerald called melancholy?). I am by now also past my twenty-second: the young man I have married is working in the family business, and there is talk of cutting down; of rationalising a firm so long gone into recession that Henry Green's claim on his book jackets that he is both industrialist and novelist seems harder and harder to justify. (It's said of Henry that his rare visits to the George Street office of Pontifex are spent in drinking gin and in shooting pigeons out of the window. Can it be that Henry is also lacking in this important quality, responsibility?) At weekends the young man and I go sometimes to stay with people in the country, and even on weekdays we go out – this seeming extraordinary as his work is exhausting. I, who have spent all day doing nothing – the imitation of my parents' life, on £2,000 a year, is exact, for we have a nanny, a young Scots girl, plus a cook and a daily cleaner – am selfishly infuriated by his tiredness, and by my own incomprehension of the workings of this engineering firm which takes up so much of his time. I am heading for a life as Madame Bovary; but that Emma had at least the conventions of her time and milieu to fight against and I have none. Most of the older couples in the world to which we appear naturally to belong are casually or seriously engaged with someone else. There is a sense of meaninglessness in the London of the time: the struggle of the Fifties to return to the Thirties has on the whole been lost and there has come the two-car family and an abundance of machines. People are assured they live in an age of unequalled prosperity. But the class horror that is England is if anything more visible now that efforts are made to narrow the gap: people who canvass for the Tories at the election appear to bear no relation to those in estates, a word so carefully chosen for its gentility but serving only, in the end, to underline the difference between the background of the canvasser, his duck-shooting estate behind him, and themselves.

So I know only that I am restless and that, as with my grandmother's generation, I have time in plenty to complain about the help. This, in the case of Ziller, was unavoidable, for Ziller, the immense German who arrived from some mysterious source at our flat in Cheyne Walk and almost immediately moved his boyfriend into the attic room beside his, was to prove the catalyst for my final bid for freedom, my escape to Rome. — As I say, I have no idea who provided Ziller: possibly my actor friend Peter Eyre, whose aunt Princess Rospigliosi ran an employment agency where girls named Pina and Maria, fresh out of Italy, sat uncomprehendingly as potential employers mouthed their necessities: clean baths, stock up the lavatory paper, food cooked anew each day, not heated up in the eternal ragù. Maybe Ziller came from there – or from a high-aspiring niece of Dig's, a butler expert who thought I should emulate her grand way of life. — One way or another, Ziller's brooding presence on the stairs, the sense of his – and his friend Edouard's – disgust at my sex, and worse, my pregnancy, had made me jump at Judy's invitation to the island in the river. — I and the young man I had married had gone north and seen a small house outside Leeds – what was it I feared there most? My own company, the fearfulness of one who cannot assume responsibility for all the most important things in life? Why did I need all these people in my flat, to render me even more useless than before? The obstacles to independence seemed insuperable, then, for I could not cook or clean or iron.

'Oakley Street is famously the most depressing street in the world,' says Peter Eyre, who is fair and long-faced, sensitive to the point of transparency. 'At least you're out of there, away from the smell of death.' (Thus we refer to Elizabeth, the religious fanatic who lived in the basement and had not been mentioned by Isobel Strachey, our landlady.) I agree

I'm grateful; Elizabeth's visits to my ground-floor bedroom, bible in hand, had filled me with 'apprehensions', as Peter rightly calls those tremors which afflict the well-off and unemployed. But Ziller . . . Peter and I sit in the drawing-room at 8 Cheyne Walk and giggle at the Prussian presence of the enormous butler – who will at the stroke of six go into the tiny kitchen behind the drawing-room, prepare a tasteless but perfect dinner, and then, on the stroke of eight, send it juddering up in the little lift we have copied from Henry and Dig's house. The food will jump up out of the floor in the room above next to our bedroom – a room I have had papered in red dragged wallpaper in order for it to make a convincing dinning-room; as Ziller comes ponderously up the stairs and hands the dinner from the dumb waiter in white cotton gloves it is impossible not to feel alarmed and to burst out laughing at the same time. 'It's hopeless,' Peter says. 'Why don't you get an Italian? But go and stay with Judy first . . .' — I never knew what the young man I had married thought of any of these arrangements: domestic life in Trevor Place had been patchy, perhaps, with various nationalities coming and going; and besides, his mind was on the closing down of the George Street offices and the Birmingham factory which had inspired his father's masterpiece, *Living*.

It is somehow known I am not delighted with the prospect of a prison sentence in a house outside Leeds – even Judy's brisk 'You'll make friends at the university there' sounds unconvincing, as I sit, happy to be back in the morgue, on the long white sofa with its scatter of bruised cushions, in the Isola Tiberina in

Rome. What shall we do tonight? Hear the story of Natalie, the thin French girl who carts her children to Ostia each day in the blazing heat to swim and picnic, anxious but uncomplaining at the strain of her life married to Sandrino, editor of the *Corriere della Sera*? Have dinner out of doors in Trastevere with Alvise and Betty de Robillant? Natalie will ask me to stay in France – I know the ache for freedom, I will accept; and Judy says, as if it's the most natural thing in the world, 'Go and stay with the de Noailles, their house is the Maison de Pompadour, in the forest at Fontainebleau, you can go on to Paris and see Henri then if you want, too . . .' How can I, offered such excitement, refuse?

I have no sense of responsibility for the simple reason that there are no responsibilities I actually have to take care of. My father and mother make sure the flat runs well in my absence, whether I'm in Rome or in the forest of Fontainebleau where I did indeed go, to a house untouched – or so it seemed to me – since Madame de Pompadour had gone there for one of the hunting parties she loved to arrange for Louis XV. My family has been absorbed into my parents': I am still a girl after all; but a girl with a child, and a wardrobe of clothes for all the smart dinners and house parties to which I insist on dragging the increasingly silent and mournful young man I met in Oxford and married over a cup of espresso coffee. I am prone to infatuations – the 'Henri' mentioned by Judy is my latest: a married man who is the bearer of a name as old as the Pompadours' and thus ripe for my snobbish love. 'So likely!' snorts Judy when I say I want to marry Henri and live on his seigneurial

estates in France. 'He's paid for by his wife's family –
and he doesn't even like women. Pull yourself
together, for heaven's sake!' But in a fantasy where I
am not only a girl but a kind of boy/girl (I know
myself attractive to what were then 'queers' or, in the
case of Judy's slang, 'corks', and imagine they can see
the lovely youth beneath my apparently female
form), I refuse to listen to her. Judy, endlessly
generous, gives me new ball gowns and encourages
my aim to be all things to all – or, as it seems, all
preponderantly homosexual – men. I'm a fool, and
probably she sees it. But Judy is too kind-hearted to
talk of fag hags and, as I think to myself, I *am* a
young man, a Greek sculpture in Harrods Dior or, if
I can stand still long enough to endure the fittings,
Charlotte's imitations of *haute couture*. Swooning
with admiration at my own masculine beauty I visit
Paris in purple with a magenta silk shirt. Piaf is
singing, the theatre is packed; Henri's handsome
profile convinces me I am in the presence of the man
who will alter my life. But of course Judy is right:
Henri flatters his vanity – just as I indulge mine – by
entering into this little fling in Paris. It transpires that
a gay Sicilian duke and his young English lover are a
part of the suite booked by Henri in the Hotel Lotti.
I'm a fag hag, definitely – but they all love me,
undoubtedly they do.

Roman society may be corrupt, but I have decided
I definitely prefer it to the Young Marrieds with
whom I, and decreasingly my husband, consort.
Possibly I know already that I shall cause them
irritation by writing about them; that Henry – the
other Henry, the writer and my father-in-law – has

sown a seed that will result in my first book. Conceivably, I know they will be hurt and I have decided I don't care. ('*Hurting* – that should be the title of your next novel,' are reportedly the words of one of Henry's ex-girlfriends, after the 'romancing over a bottle of wine' has turned sour and the author of *Loving* and *Doting* has stopped seeing her.) Yet it is no more my goal to hurt people than that of most writers – I need to write, and, when I begin, the Young Marrieds must be my subjects, for I understand their frivolity, their desire for excitement, their need to exchange husbands and houses and possessions rather than moulder – as they would see it, and so would I at this point in my life – in the trappings first chosen. Novelty results in a terrible sameness. This will be, as I discuss it with a new friend, Francis (the son of Violet Wyndham, a writer himself, a son as kind as his mother to an uncertain member of a family which has itself lost its certainty), this sameness will be the theme of my book.

Judy kicks off her shoes, lights her millionth STOP, and stares anxiously at me. We have just returned from the Vice Bar – but in very different circumstances from the usual highly good-humoured return, fuelled by Bloody Marys and the famous sandwiches. This time I am ill. Judy has gripped my arm as the cab raced round the Victor Emmanuel monument, its whiteness rising all round me like a nightmare, a sea of marble where I shall be caught, homesick and lost, for ever. I have completely lost my balance. — Yet, as it happens, all my symptoms are ripe for discussion in psychoanalytic terms – not that Judy can resist being Judy when it comes to examination of what is wrong with one of her favourite 'girls'. No balance? — 'You shouldn't have come this time. You're needed at home; it's thrown you off course.' Sick? 'No wonder you feel sick, Henri is coming back to Rome tonight and there's the Volpi Ball in Venice. I didn't say you could come – but it'll be all right – we might all drive up there this evening. What's Al's phone number again? That idiot Adri has thrown away my address book . . .' Then, 'Squitters? My dear girl, I've had a spastic colon since the year dot. Don't be surprised if peas come out whole – they do when *I* go.' — A psychiatrist is even summoned – though Judy knows little of the discipline. He is young, dark, certain that my complaint is nervous. He suggests the hospital on the island; I feel a medieval fear and rightly, for the Isola Tiberina has not renovated its hospital, by the looks of it, for at least three hundred years . . . I cry to go home; reduced once again to early childhood, I demand my elder brother comes to fetch me, having forgotten I am married; though Judy, very firmly, remembers this. 'He'll come tomorrow,' she says of the poor young man who is my husband and doubt- less much regretting the fact. — Within twenty-four hours, torn from the restructuring of the family engineering firm, silent and pale, he comes. — Dizzy, retching, I am flown back to London, to see a hearse pull away from the strip of road outside 8 Cheyne Walk. I try to crack a joke, and fail. Soon, my parents are at my side and the doctor on his way. And I know, as I lie on the sofa which is by the window overlooking the Thames, that water from the river I've just left was my downfall. '*Not* very clever,' the doctor says when results come from the tests, showing hepatitis, paratyphoid and colitis. — I know myself punished, for my frothy life, my lack of care for anyone or anything other than myself. At night I dream of the kitchen, the dank, evil-smelling brick-work, the tap which brought water straight up from the Tiber into my glass. Judy's voice 'yobs' on through the dream, placing Natalie next to Alvise, pushing one 'girl' or another into the French Embassy to sit next to Nancy Mitford's most painful object of infatuation, Gaston Palewski. The Vice Bar spins, as it did that fatal day when illness came to strike: I see the black-and-white floor begin to whirl – but then, to make final mockery of my pathetic and depleted condition, the voice of my aunt Clare rings in my head, as, with her little laugh, a crossword in *The Times* on her knee, she describes the fall of a friend of hers on leaving an apartment block in London – '*measured* her length on the tessellated marble floor!' Colin, who is sitting by her, pencilling in clues, snickers encouragingly: Clare is being funny again. Is this what I have become? Someone who tells 'funny' stories, preferably of the sufferings of a friend? Mortified, I lie sweating in the throes of my illness – which, for some reason, the Viennese doctor decides to treat with little phials of something 'natural'. I take a very long time to recover and by the time I do my husband has made his home in Yorkshire and I, and my little household, are alone.

SIX

Luisa, Agnes, John McCubbin

Agnes Kabicek
as a young woman

John McCubbin

Until my twenty-third year, when I found myself in the house by the river, where the trees planted in the thin strip between the road and the Embankment seemed so close one could think oneself part of them, I had no idea that I would ever be offered employment: that I could earn (although it soon became clear I must); and that, however humbly, I could earn my living by writing about (and thus spoiling, as some said) the world I saw. — At first, I was too ill to take the advice of my friends and look for work. The ampoules, glass phials of this mysterious 'natural' product that were supposedly my cure, had to be broken three times a day and their contents ingested. — I had the strength to do little more than play with my son – and for this I preferred to go along to Ranelagh Gardens, after descending the whirl of purple lino that was the lower half of the redbrick mansion where we had bought our flat. Occasionally I met Major Heathcote, the house's owner, who resided in these lower regions, reached through a door on the half-landing. — I liked to imagine that Major Heathcote approved my outings with baby and pram (I don't remember a pushchair being a part of young mothers' lives then), and that this was simply a fantasy on the part of an insecure person in need of approval did not occur to me until much later, when Major Heathcote, businesslike and no more, offered money for the flat I left, showing, perhaps unsurprisingly, no trace of sentimental affection for the young woman whose infant carriage (as nannies called a pram in those days) was only too frequently parked in his hall.

I needed identity, and proof that I deserved respect, I suppose; and motherhood appeared to provide it. In any case, I knew well I was hardly seen as a maternal figure and no more. I was a girl, a divorced girl, it is true; and it was soon borne in on me that I must not only find employment: I must also discover suitors – one of whom would complete the broken circle caused by my own negligence and folly. It would be unthinkable, in that age, to subject a child to a loose arrangement, such as two people living together: what is needed is a husband. ('He rings to ask, has the marriage broken down irretrievably?' asks my father in a tired voice as we stand in the basement passage at Glen: my father is building a Gothic castle for my younger sister Catherine in the old dairy there and I am wandering about, unable to think what to do next. 'Yes,' I say, surprised that the young man I married and my father are in communication like this. It was the money that was being sorted out, I imagine. — 'Yes, it has.' Was this for the lawyer's benefit? But our divorce is far in the future, when the poor young man, as the law of that day requires, has to enact a parody of our Ritz honeymoon in a Brighton hotel, with a paid 'lady', tea brought in by a maid who is in turn remunerated for discovering them, fully dressed in bed, and giving her testimony in court to the night spent together.) — I must find someone, who will bring both stability and financial security to our precarious set-up by the Thames. — Yet, as I am soon to learn, suitors are themselves more precarious for a girl with familial requirements: they come and go, and as they are not permitted to stay under the roof they bear little resemblance to Penelope's famous suitors, except in their ability, demonstrated in the earlier phase also, to eat and drink and carouse generally until dawn. They may propose, but they are soon discouraged when they learn I have the shroud of my marriage to unpick. No one it seems, is prepared to commit to the role of stepfather and instigator of a new family; and those who are, are for one reason or another sent away.

The arrival of Luisa Durso from Italy transpires to be an echo, at first, and ludicrously, not detected by myself, of my own easily mocked situation – that is, in need of paid employment and also, despite the fact that my criteria fail to be met by the few importunate suitors, in search of a paterfamilias for the upper maisonette at 8 Cheyne Walk. Luisa is from Positano, in the shin of Italy. She is dark, quick-witted and already plump, a harbinger of the great weight which a lifetime of cooking – for her family, for London Society, for anyone who wants her – will bring to her and end her life. She will scorch garlic in a pan with hastily tossed pasta – Bolognese and Napolitana are residents, soon, of the watery flat, with its grey English river view – and she will push me into entertaining, with her ready scorn for a hostess (as she wishes me to be) who does not have guests at her table constantly. Luisa soon becomes Sancha Panza to my Donna Quixote: she is at my side as I charge at the windmills provided by my new, single existence: 'Emma Yorke' – a good name for a socially pushing girl, with its murmur of the eighteenth-century nobility and distant counties, all the unchanging snobberies of England require. Fame will come to Luisa, who does indeed become extremely well known – for her wit, her incredible speed (red cabbage in ten minutes; poached salmon and mayonnaise before you can turn round); and who feels free to show her contempt for a person such as myself, who vacillates between one possibility and another, and in most cases loses them all. — The nanny, a blank-faced young woman with frizzy hair tied back in a bun, hates Luisa and leaves me notes complaining and telling tales; a plate of liver is brought triumphantly down from the nursery as proof that Luisa is trying, by overfeeding her, to hasten her end. — Nannies come and go. Luisa stays.

We are in a year of births and deaths; and, in the case of my parents' household, straightforward vanishings; for no sooner have they suffered the agonising drawn-out end of my aunt Clare in the Walnut Room at Glen and returned to London than John McCubbin, for many years dependably *in situ*, whether with Agnes Kabicek in the upper reaches of 6 Swan Walk or in the basement at Glen, with his latest companion, disappears without leaving a word or even a demand that letters be forwarded on to him. Agnes is red-eyed and pepper goes without restraint into the soup, choking my mother's friends and bringing an odd, puzzled expression to my father's face. A litter of kittens (they come from my son's cat: somehow they have fetched up in my parents' house) play in his dressing-room, where once John's neatly rolled arrangements of my father's socks had lain on the narrow bed, used only in times of illness (which is never); the kittens jump and then fall in make-believe faints around my father's waste basket, and in the careful drawers where his clothes are laid out. — John is missed elsewhere too: I am not actually living there so cannot miss his 'egg-but-no-bacon' and triumphant flourish as the dish is set on the breakfast table, but I miss the daily visits to my flat, whether to mend a plug that has fused (I am helpless in this department also) or to collect me and whisk me to a party if it is raining and Charlotte's lilac shantung is in danger of getting wet. — My mother says John had muttered about going to see his brother; we are all silent, envisaging the twin we can't believe in: but what rises before the eye is a double of John McCubbin, grim-faced in Glasgow as his absconding brother falls on his charity. But why?

Still recovering from the treble attack dealt me by the waters of the Tiber, I dream at night of glass tubes and strange monsters; and in my dreams I visit the 'other' house, the house of my father's first family, as if I am searching for the truth about the lost John there – as if the answer can lie in this rambling, shabby house on Campden Hill where my father's first wife Pamela was placed at the time of their divorce. — I have been there, but not often. Pamela – all I know of her is that she was chosen by my father's mother as a suitable bride and that her own mother, adventurous and imperious, had rescued governesses from the ravages of the Russian Revolution but spent all her time in England in bed – Pamela is kind and vague, head stuck forward like a tortoise, a pretty woman whose failure in love has encouraged her to assume the look of old age. It has been said to me that this first wife of my father had liked to emulate her mother, and took to her bed; that he had, on leaving one day for America, threatened her with the ending of their marriage if he should find her in bed when he returned; she was; and he divorced her. I don't know the truth of this, though the story was frightening. — It was many years later that I learned of Pamela's cleverness, for she had been one of the few female undergraduates at Cambridge in the 1920s. I remember going to Hill Lodge, as this fine but neglected Regency house in Holland Park is called, and finding her in a state of indignation that I was not 'allowed' to learn Hebrew at my school, when it had not crossed my mind to want to. Was Pamela, as some people made out, 'dotty' – or, by surprising with her strange claims and remarks, simply showing she could not be so easily forgotten, deposited in this house that smelt of crumbs and all the vicar's tea parties she felt bound, in so large a dwelling, to give? — No one can know; possibly I dreamt of her because I had known my aunt Clare shortly before her death and had wondered what life at Glen had been like when my father was married to Pamela – before the bed episode, before he then met my mother and I was born. Had Clare, who enjoyed my new worldliness as she lay dying (I brought her gin and gossiped in my grown-up way of the smart people I knew in London), got on better with Pamela than she did with her present sister-in-law? But I could hardly see that this could be the case. Pamela was lacking in worldliness, the one quality my aunt appreciated.

Neither of the women my father had married would have provided distraction for my aunt that summer, and I think sometimes that her death must have been lonely, when I was the only one to bring in rumours and tired scandal to the sickroom. For my mother, in a totally different way from her predecessor, was not a *mondaine* either – and my mother's father, 'the colonel', as Lieutenant-Colonel George Powell was known, trembled and shook so violently at the approaching demise of my aunt that John's laughter in the dining-room at Glen was almost uncontainable.

In my dream where I search for the missing John in Pamela's untended house of relics, escapees and half-forgotten children, I see a man who is and is not my father and I see him walk into the delightful little oval sitting-room that was Pamela's own. A young woman rises to greet him; she is not Pamela, but I know somehow she is another of my father's wives. He comes towards her. — I wake, as a small child pulls at my hand, and think it my son, creeping down from his room above in my flat that overlooks the river. But the child is a dream son or brother; the new wife fades and day comes in through bright curtains; I have dreamt, I am obscurely aware, of birth. — Indeed, births came that year both before and after Clare died in my father's arms in the room at Glen where I had as a child found all the family secrets. Colin's second son was born that year. He had the features of the family and the pale colour of his mother. — In that year also, the mystery of the disappearance of John McCubbin was finally solved. Birth lay at the root

111

of it – and I saw that not one of us had taken the trouble to understand the plight of those involved.

'If only women knew how much men hate them.' Gore Vidal, in Rome: I visit once again, eager for an exciting time, as well as a feeling I am far away from England, which seems as deeply mired in the ideas and prejudices of the past as a gentleman's club. The literary world has welcomed *Lucky Jim* but appears to coast along, still satisfied with its smug, pseudo-aristocratic view of itself: Gore is a bracing change from all this, an exciting time in himself – and, best of all for me, unobtainable. He and his friend Howard have moved to live here; Gore walks up from the Campo dei Fiori to lunch at Judy's; the morgue jumps with the sudden laughter Gore's outrageous wit provokes. As we eat Adri's pasta (as careless as Luisa's – but Adri sulks if she's not complimented and Luisa wears a sardonic expression as the food goes down, as if a long stint in the kitchens of the Borgias lies behind her and she can only pity the guests who eat so trustingly), Gore talks of politics in America – of people I don't know and never will – and I feel, not for the first time, the full extent of my ignorance. If only I could marry someone like Gore – or indeed why not Gore himself? Soon, with the arrival of more wine and a serious settling down on the part of Judy to ashtray and attendant STOP, a possible union is under discussion: Gore will run for President and I –

naturally – will be First Lady of this mysterious country to which I feel I will one day belong. There! – it's done. Caught in the spell of charm, fame and endless possibilities I forget my actual situation: an overdraft which is proving worrying to my father, a flat and a small child and – in a phrase I have always appreciated – no visible means of support. — I won't be married to this handsome, talented writer, of course – but just for one afternoon, on the island with the dreamer's temple buried under the cobbles, I can think that I will be. — Certainly, it would be better than a future in London, where nothing is un-predictable. The Sixties (the real Sixties, where change blows through with a violence that takes people by the scruff of the neck and either destroys or radically alters them) badly needs to happen.

When the afternoon is over and Gore has gone, I feel the emptiness. Why do I know so little? What can I do to show there is something, after all, buried, like the shrine to Aesculapius in the Piazza, under the flippant, stony heart I appear to have developed since I was old enough to go out in the world? What *is* the world? Can I go on interminably, listening to Judy 'yob' the Colonnas and the Pecci-Blunts and Henri – or Corks de B, as she refers to him? Will it always be fascinating and 'amusing' – the term used by the international set, who are unamused if they are not on the *Creole*, Niarchos's yacht, in the waters of the Aegean, or skiing down the slopes at Gstaad, or dancing in London's newest clubs for the rich. 'Is it amusing in London?' asks a Brandolini or a Caracciolo or an Agnelli. By now I want to tell them to call when I get back and I'll look out of the window and let them know. — Meeting Gore and my fantasy proposal has made me realise how far I am from achieving anything in life. As if to underline the frivolity of my existence, Judy has given me a white truffle grater as a present. Luisa, on the decreasing sums awarded her for household shopping, will turn up her nose at such a luxury item and give her mocking laugh. If, that is, when I return to London, Luisa is still there. My conscience is bad, the 'fun' I am enjoying at Judy's begins to turn to ashes in my mouth. For Luisa, before I left, had handed me a bill for taking a taxi to do the shopping: I had expressed astonishment; and she had announced her imminent departure from the flat.

I should have waited, on the purple lino half-landing, where Luisa handed me the piece of paper with its crazy sums. Of course, there is something wrong; but as so often before, I am too keen to get to the airport to listen to the truth.

The letter comes when I'm back in the flat, Luisa gone and a victorious (as she believes) nanny coping with cooking her own food and that of my son. What a useless person I am, I think – and not for the first time: useless at understanding others or in performing even the simplest chore. How can I censure the smart set in Rome when I am myself no more than a faintly ridiculous – and now penniless – echo of them? Luisa's letter, in a strange mix of English and Italian, informs me she is going to have a baby. John McCubbin is the dad. John's disappearance is explained. — My conscience grows worse, for Luisa has gone too, but most definitely not to be with him. — Luisa had come from Italy, to find a husband and father for her children: I had gone there, apparently, for the same purpose (or so my ridiculous proposal in Rome seemed to suggest). I am alone in my flat, with my son; Luisa struggles somewhere, awaiting hers. (But John McCubbin plays the trump card in this situation, as so proficient a fire-engine driver might be expected to do. At the birth of Luisa's child he appears from nowhere and goes straight to the hospital. He looks in at the child in its crib. 'I claim it,' he announces to the astounded nurses.) And he does: with the speed of one of Luisa's makeshift soufflés, John and his new bride are together, Luisa cooking in my parents' kitchen and John laughing with renewed vigour in his stance in front of the sideboard, behind my father's chair. Agnes has retired.

SEVEN

The Marble Bottom

Emma Tennant in the mid 1960s

'If only women knew how much men hate them' –
Vidal's saying (appropriated since and made banal by
Germaine Greer) turns out to be prophetic, as far as
my continued determination not to find satisfaction is
concerned. — The hatred, if such it is, clearly
fascinates me. It is infinitely preferable to its opposite,
'love', of which I have a well-founded suspicion, for
we are in the age before the rising-up of women
against men; the age of Norman Mailer's 'Time of
Her Time', a story demonstrating the power of man
to subjugate woman by reason of sheer sexual
magnetism. Hatred is clear-cut, crisp and seductive.
The mistake I make, at this crucial juncture, is to
imagine that hatred will best be found in homosexual
men, when the buried homosexuals – that is, virtually
all heterosexual men – are those with
an ambition to maim and scar. — I had already,
before Vidal's observation, gone in search of those so
far removed from contemplating loving women that
to capture them would be the equivalent of the
successful ending of a fable or fairy tale, the finding
of the black tulip, the triumphant awakening from a
dream with the butterfly seen there in one's hand.
Bruce Chatwin, first sighted at the Villa d'Este near
Padua, was one such: more were to follow. — But the
villa, rented by the rich young painter, the diminutive
Teddy Millington-Drake, was a perfect setting for the
chase, the near-success, the final falling-back. Bruce,
known as 'Chatwina' to the many other homosexual

men I shall come to know, was ensconced upstairs in bed, suffering from jaundice. The lion – for this, already, he clearly is – is brought low and immobile: I mount the stairs, on the evening of my arrival at this shabby villa, with its red damask walls and enticing statuary and dripping pools, to meet him whether my host will have it or not. — My son is with me on this trip and we have come from Venice, hardly suitable for a two-and-a-half-year-old; we have sat in a gondola and he has stared uncomprehendingly at the Giudecca and waited politely in Florian's for an ice-cream. The sordid, over-done melancholy, the sense of death and underlying hysteria of Venice, the smart people at Cipriani's and the travellers with their knapsacks and bewildered wanderings over bridges and by the side of slime-filled canals, have made me ready for an encounter with Bruce. — Not that I knew of him, apart from jokes by Christopher Gibbs, an apricot-haired antiquary, a friend who will move into my flat in Cheyne Walk and look after things when I go away. I know Bruce has the keenest eye at Sotheby's; that he is preposterously young; and that he is a friend of Teddy's, the mournful beneficiary of his mother's wealth. That Bruce was at the Villa d'Este I had no idea.

'You can't go up to see Bruce,' said Teddy in the cross, quavering voice which meant there was a faint chance he might laugh. 'He has jaundice and then you'll catch it and so will the little boy.'

Of course, I go. The Italian air of endless post-ponement of meals and coffee dawdled over in the soft afternoons and evenings at the Villa d'Este have not yet penetrated my resolve – which is, as if I have developed a hunter's instinct since the sad débâcle of my ended marriage and my own short-handed manner with any who might propose a sensible life, to conquer the unconquerable: to find the price of rejection in the most unexpected places. — I can sense, as I mount the crumbling staircase, that my instinct may prove to be right. Someone awaits me who is truly, ravishingly, impossible to seduce.

By the time I meet Chatwin, he is, as it turns out, as ready to meet me as I him. Bright yellow in the face, round head propped against a pillow in the French Empire *bateau-lit* where Teddy has put him to see out the disease, he resembles a Germanic folk-tale hero, a grown-up Hansel who has leapt from the cage where the wicked witch imprisoned him and has come into the world determined never to stray in the forest again. — This time, Bruce knows where he is going. We talk, and talk and talk. Meals come and go, in the sombre little dining-room; a friend of Teddy's (female) provides company for him and it is hard to say he feels jealousy, when nearly all his facial expressions suggest the imminent discovery of something disagreeable. Bruce, as I soon discover, knows everything; that I know nothing appears to excite him rather than the reverse: he is a show-off and a brilliant one. Chatwin knows the world; he knows the corruption of the big art houses; he loves men, parts of men, and in this case, as I find the reason for his visit to his lover Teddy's rented house, he loves and covets a certain white marble bottom, Greek, sixth century BC, the broken-off posterior of a kouros. He loves the narrow hips, the beauty that has never been matched, of a sculpted youth from shores where men went mad, dreaming of athletes. As Bruce speaks, I take on, or try, the colours and contours of the desires he manifests; thus, possibly, I can divine his sexuality. Bruce is a man with no woman in him, no wish for women either. Yet, to my extreme delight, I see he is ready to meet the challenge. Back in England, he will be mine. He understands that even in illness he is irresistible – or so his bright eyes and shrieking laugh seem to say.

We drive, Teddy at the wheel, myself behind him and a still-yellow Chatwin talking and talking, to a house that is, like all I see since falling under his spell, a house in a dream: Palladian, on the River Brenta, built for sadness, solipsism and the delights of melancholy. — I am told this is the Villa Malcontenta; the exotic name, the sheer impossibility of translation (where and how in England could the white pillars and rotunda and the name: Misery Hall, Villa Discontent, exist? Perhaps in the fancy of a satirist such as Peacock but never with the deadly seriousness accomplished here). We are taken in, past weeping willows to the hall. It's a white, overcast day which shows with a bilious light the frescos on the whitewashed stairwell; it grows darker as we ascend; finally we are in the presence of an old man, the owner Bertie Lansberg. — What does Bruce do, to secure his prize? I remember only an interminable wait, with Teddy's small figure, very dapper as ever in a dark linen jacket, wandering around the artefacts and pictures, sighing as if once again disappointed; and I thought he looked as happy as I had seen him, in this temple to disaffection, indifference, accidie. We were brought no refreshments. — Eventually, bearing the marble bottom before him and partially obscured by the buttocks, his bare arms joining the torso broken off at the top of the thigh giving the object an illusion of being larger than it actually was, Bruce appears. We follow him down the stairs, a nervous footman vanishing silently into the recesses of the gloomy hall as we descend. There is no sign of Bertie Lansberg. Has he given the treasured behind to Bruce? Or did Bruce steal it? Does the proprietor of this temple to sadness think it will be sold for him at Sotheby's, fortunes given for a piece of marble statue, replica of a youth who lived when Homer was still fresh in memory and before the death of Pan? Whatever he may think, it's in Chatwin's possession now. I see it a year later, exhibited behind glass in his tiny London flat. I wonder, sometimes, if there will be an international scandal, such as erupts from time to time in the art world.

The nature of Chatwin is ephemeral – so that, on return to London, to the necessity of finding a job, to nursery schools for my son, it is almost impossible to summon him to mind. Possibly as a result of his exciting talk, the non-existence of an education begins more and more to grieve and annoy me. — I had told my mother at the time, in a tone of such firmness that she had found herself unable to reply, that I had no intention of staying at St Paul's beyond the age of fifteen. — I had left; I had 'gone to Paris' as girls of my kind so often in those days did, really to fill in before the coming-out ball and then, if all has gone well, the wedding day. Now, demanding of my father that he invest £4,000 in a country retreat so that I could go away and study in peace, I found myself in Chute Standen, not far from Andover in Hampshire. Piles of books came with me, and a large brown radio. There was a garden, an orchard and, at the bottom of the gentle hill on which the village was set out, a pub. — It was not long, however, before the volumes of Plato and Nietzsche proved intractable. Staying so long on my own, to which I was not accustomed, produced a buzzing in the ears; and I was drawn to walk down to the inn, friendly as I thought, sometimes taking my son with me. Friends came to Baker's Cottage, as the thick-walled, thatched little house was known, and the books went almost untouched, for I have no memory of any of them wishing to discuss Plato or Nietzsche. When there was company, the place was enjoyable – though Sunday, with its dull green rural aspect, would sometimes lead me to rush back to London, dis-countenancing those who, like Mark Boxer (he and his wife Arabella were guests), had let friends stay in their London house and had nowhere to return to. — I was determined to read; and I did, helped by my most widely read friend, Francis: I read Henry James, all of Proust, Dickens and Beckett and Joyce (but most often Henry James, to whose way of thought I became so acclimatised that a few years later, when I was to meet the descendant of a fortune-hunter who had inspired Gilbert Osmond, wicked seducer of Isobel Archer in *Portrait of a Lady*, I knew what I would find). I began to try and write and, again helped by Francis, I thought of the people I knew – as he did, some of them well: those Young Marrieds and vacant rich who were to figure in the novel. — Francis it was, with Mark Boxer, who found me work at *Queen* magazine. From 8 Cheyne Walk I would travel the world – an unnatural occupation, perhaps, for a woman with a child and no husband, who had to keep her household ticking over. But that was the job: Travel Editor; if I lacked Chatwin's wide-ranging knowledge, I had just as much of a sense of adventure as he, or so I told myself — As if determined to show myself equal to the task, I booked myself first to go to the southern coast of Turkey. I knew there was an amphitheatre there at Termessos, undiscovered at that time, pure Chatwin country — and I, in my guise as handsome young man, nomad, wanderer, would walk the ruins above Antalya and send back my account of it to *Queen*.

Queen magazine – before it merged with *Harper's* and became what it is today, a run-of-the-mill glossy magazine without the glamour of *Vogue* – had, at the time of my going there, recently been bought by Jocelyn Stevens, nephew and heir of Sir Edward Hulton. The cast list (for at first it seemed to resemble a novel or play, and an unusual one at that) or rather, the group on the masthead and the contributors, were talented and free to do as they pleased. Mark Boxer designed the pages; Francis called in the likes of Colin MacInnes to write on whatever they thought up together. A benevolent Beatrix Miller presided as Editor; and, in the upper chamber, a Bluebeard who sent messages of piercing ferocity to the many girls who worked for him, was Jocelyn, popularly known as the Boss. — It was the birth, I suppose, of Antonioni's Sixties, as shown in his film *Blow-Up*. David Bailey, of angelic beauty, ran in and out of the tall building in Fetter Lane. Criminals mixed with the new aristocracy of talent exploding from regions where it had for so long, by reason of class and snobbery, been repressed. — From this scene I came and went. Inaugural flights – a kind of torment, as planes packed with travel agents, all male, descended on holiday resorts and expected my happy participation in the boozing and knees-up which were a part of the free trip. Africa – I read my way around the source of the Nile, so maddened by the 'correspondents' that devouring Aldous Huxley seemed preferable to hearing their comments on the repetitive plains, the endless and identical panoramas of bush, giraffe and antelope. The beauty and isolation Chatwin craved – and described – were certainly not here. — Apart from Turkey, where I suffered from the attentions of the government-appointed guide (a danger I might have envisaged if I had given it a thought), I was always surrounded by others. My desire to escape was thwarted. When I returned to London it was indeed to isolation: for I knew by now how badly I lacked a companion, a lover, someone who would simply be there when I was – and, most important, be there when I wasn't, for I had a strong sense that I must go and find somewhere else to live. London was circumscribed, for a girl with little education and therefore few prospects beyond the travel pages of a glossy magazine. I was invited to spend an evening with a Duke who, on sitting me down in a restaurant (L'Escargot) fired straight off with 'What are my chances?' No point in wasting time. The evening, progressing to the Stork Room and the desperate wit of Al Burnett ('She was only a fisherman's daughter but when she saw his rod she reeled'), the whisky in coffee cups, and the dead roses brought round by exhausted cigarette girls, answered the question all by itself. A coffin of arum lilies arrived the next morning, but I'm already gone – to Rome, to Madrid, to another 'safari' where hippos gazed balefully at the journalists as the sun went down. — On one occasion, slumped miserably over the bottle of champagne an inept seducer expected me to drink before giving a favourable assessment of his chances, I simply fell asleep. On another, taken out with clearly serious intentions by Jacob Rothschild – he would today be termed a baby banker – it was the other way around: the future millionaire, keen to preserve his mental agility for a day of financial gambling ahead, elected to drop me home at nine at night, saying he had to be in bed by ten. I am bored, restless; the only pleasure lies in those days at the office when one scandal or another bursts to the surface; or one of the girls, heavily chained in gold as all were at that time, sobs loudly on the fashion floor at the arrival of a directive from above: the Boss notes that gold chains worn by the girls are too long and bump against the desks. He insists they are shortened. — Mark, who is the most exciting design editor of his time, lays out the dazzling pages; Francis, frivolous when he pleases, supplies the caption 'It's All White, Jacqueline' – we all laugh; B. Miller smiles and sighs wistfully at her own ability to allow everyone to do exactly as they please.

The characters in my novel, whether I know it or not, begin to present themselves. I go to Paris and fall in love with a dark beauty, a man so slender he is almost etiolated; a man of secret music (I never could discover the name of the haunting songs he had on repeat on his record player, in his day-and-night curtained room in the rue du Bac). I eat *oursins*, digging into the broken-open prickly globe and pulling out the orange-pink mouthfuls, a substitute for the sex the beauty denies me as we lie night after night in his four-poster, he drenched in scent (Guerlain's *Heure Bleu*) and clothed from head to toe in silk. He will be my mysterious lover, in the novel, the man my discontented young housewives want to love them; and, like me, they will fail in their aspirations. — I travel back and forth, transported by the infatuation I believe I feel for him. One day, without warning, and in the tradition of the best of these moonshiny affairs, the doors to the rue du Bac apartment are locked and – to Tangier? to America? – he has gone. Acting the part of the abandoned girl, I walk the bridges of Paris, satisfactorily it rains as in the movies, and – although with difficulty – I weep in my attic room in the rue des Grands Augustins.

On the cover of *The Colour of Rain*, as you can see, is a group of smart young mothers and nannies of the time. Osbert Lancaster has drawn them; he is illustrating the lives – and bouffant hair-styles, bee-hives as they are known – of the world I have, since my marriage and separation, been in. Henry Vyner has married Margaret, a beauty whom he decks out with rubies like fat red steaks, dangling from her earlobes and her neck and wrists. Antonia, who has married Hugh Fraser, has transformed herself into a real beauty, and everyone, in life as in my novel, is in love with her. Ingrid, cousin of both Francis and myself changes husbands in the book – again, as she does in life, moving in her case also between cousins, from Jonathan Guinness to Paul Channon. Everyone has money, most have small children. Into their world comes the dark young man from the rue du Bac.

It was said of Fred Warner, an immensely tall man who lived in London, in those chambers known as Albany in the heart of Piccadilly, an impeccably English address which he nevertheless made seem foreign, exotic, slightly suspect, that he was a spy. He was the Third Man – so the story went – and certainly he had been a friend of the rebarbative (to some) and charming Guy Burgess; but, as the years passed and actual third, fourth, fifth men, etc. were excitedly discovered, Fred dropped to the back of the queue and continued to live his life as before – which is to say, again, impeccably but with a suspect quality which was hard to define. The Third Man slur lost him advancement in the Foreign Office – when I knew him he had lingered in Greece as First Secretary at the British Embassy; and shortly, as if in punishment for past sins, he was to be appointed Ambassador in Laos. But there was no knowing, so deep was the mystery surrounding Fred, whether he did not perhaps enjoy this posting – out of the way, a country belonging to the extraordinary books of Norman Lewis (but of course by the time he got there, in the process of being destroyed by US bombs)

– more than, say, Paris or Rome. — From the moment we met I saw a teacher, for he was immensely well read and knowledgeable; somehow, repeating my mistaken desires for unattainable men, I saw also a type of father/husband figure, highly suitable for the age of girlitude, who would effect a kind of Pygmalion transformation on me. I would become both a handsome young man (I always knew instinctively when this was what was most wished for, on the part of my prey) and yet also an ambassadress, entertaining graciously in foreign capitals, fascinating visiting dignitaries with the new learning my husband had imparted to me. — The fantasy grew apace; I decided not to confide it until after we had travelled round the north of Greece together; and duly, when Fred arrived to meet me in the bar of the Hotel Grande Bretagne in Athens – to my mind then the most glamorous place on earth – I kept quiet about my matrimonial intentions and downed a Tom Collins and ate a packet of pistachio nuts without giving myself away.

'We're going to Suli,' announces Fred, who seems taller than ever when surrounded by Greek shipping magnates in the bar. 'The Suliot women were the bravest women in history, throwing themselves one by one in a dancing chain off a high cliff rather than be captured by the Turks.' And he laughs, looking like a brigand as he does so; as mysterious as the rest of him, the laugh is both provocative and collusive, as if the listener, just discovered to be equally a spy, a covert communist (as I always thought Fred to be) must join in the mirth at this shared joke concerning the illegal activities on which both have embarked. —

More like Trelawney than Byron, Fred has a wildness
of imagination impossible to envisage being allowed
out in the bureaucratic circles in which he moves. I
feel sure at all times that he is just about to be found
out – for what I don't know – and sent to walk the
plank or languish in a foreign jail. — It is therefore
vital, for his own respectability and progress (this he
as much as concedes) for him to marry. A girl of my
kind, even if already married and therefore a
divorced woman by the time I can go to the altar, will
be ideal for Fred. — We set off for the north of the
Peloponnese in high spirits, Fred promising to
introduce me to *sipurro*, the strongest and purest
alcohol to be found in mountain villages, and to
show me the Byzantine churches of Metéora, then
almost unknown to the public at large: churches high
on pointed pinnacles of rock. Fred will charm the
monks who live their hermits' lives there, with his
caressing use of the demotic Greek and his courteous
acceptance of squares of *loukoumi*, the Turkish
delight invariably handed out with thimbles of ouzo
and tiny cups of *vari glyko* (very sweet as I believed it
to mean) coffee. In the great dusty libraries perched
high above the temptations of the world, I stare
admiringly at Fred as he answers the personal
questions Greeks, whether *papas* or laymen, feel
compelled to ask. How old are you? Fred says he is
saranda tessera; with my rudimentary grasp of the
language I understand the sharp inquisition that
follows: How old is the young lady? Twenty-four?
Are you her father/brother? . . . The temptation to
bring forward my dashing proposal of marriage
grows as I sip the ouzo and watch the basket lowered

for the old monk's provisions as it goes slowly down the sheer rock face to the waiting novice on the ground. — The air at this altitude is intoxicating; we stand on the terrace of the monastery at Ossios Loukas that evening, looking out, and we smell the sharp resin from forests of pines hundreds of feet below. All of Greece appears to lie before us, Delphi on the side of the mountain we have visited this afternoon, where the priestesses of the oracle could, or so I cannot resist imagining, divine the mystery of any incomer, even Fred. (But by then the *sipurro*, procured with deftness from the most unpromising village shop – a shop appearing to sell only bales of striped ticking, ironmongery, and blue notebooks faded by the sun – has begun to take effect.) — We are appointed a cell each, in this most civilised of monasteries. It is out of season and we are the only guests – or incumbents, as it begins to seem as sleepless hour follows sleepless hour. It has not occurred to my companion, obviously, to visit me in my cell. Perhaps I see then the possible disadvantages of the fantasy life I have concocted for myself.

Nothing, however, appears to deflect me from my complicated gender-switching, as it would be known today: I am determined to be the man my birth denied me, and Fred, enjoying this travesty of maleness which I assume whenever I can, gives me a book, of about 1860 and most certainly not since reprinted, which concerns the adventures of a young woman and her illicit visit to Mount Athos. 'First, cut off my breasts,' this illuminating text begins. Later, enfolded in a Turkish rug, our transformed heroine is carried into the monastery in the southern

Peloponnese where even hens are forbidden, so total is the interdiction on the female in any shape or form. — I think of Bruce Chatwin and feel that the spareness, freedom for deep concentration and avoidance of feminine frippery would be perfect for him there. — But at this stage in my life I am blind to the frivolity and superficiality of most men: concerned only with my own ignorance and ability to be charmed away from the serious by the ephemeral, I consider woman – as do most women and nearly all men at that time – the epitome of meaninglessness, worthy only of shopping or giving birth. — I stand by the River Lethe and listen to Fred's tales of ancient Greece, the legends and the wars and the gods of whom I know so little. Forgetfulness, so he told me, will come if I drink of this muddy water, which trickles at my feet between unprepossessing banks. — Even I have read Keats, at the school I was too lazy to attend after the age of fifteen; but I have no need of these waters, for, as I admit to Fred as he stands laughing at me, I have forgotten practically everything I learned there already. — We go to Dodona, and wait in the oak groves for the sound of the gong, beaten by the priestess in her appeal to Zeus. But the sense of any woman once there has long deserted the place: the scholarship of Bowra or Finlay and German archaeology rule in the place of nymphs or mad women, the maenads who rushed down the hillside, drunk on black wine, and tore men and horses limb from limb. I take my copy of Thucydides back to the car Fred hired for the trip, which is nearly over now; I am not even half way through the Peloponnesian Wars and, once again, feel someone

133

has sneaked me a beaker of the waters of Lethe. One of the greatest drawbacks, as I discover when in the company of the clever, compassionate and classically educated (but not woman-loving) men I choose to be with, is a gradual and then accelerating decrease in self-confidence. What indeed is my point? Even Greek lessons when I return to London fail to bolster a sense of myself (I want to be able to walk like Fred, long-legged, instantly popular, in the villages of Greece and make friends. I don't want to take the hospitality, at that time freely offered and frequently impoverishing to the giver, without at least being able to say thank you in the demotic).

In London, in my drawing-room at 8 Cheyne Walk, I propose to Fred: there are several other people there but no one hears me. He says he will give his answer in a week; like an envoy to an ancient court I wait (knowing of course, as I must do, that this is another plan that cannot succeed). But Fred is willing to play the game. I am summoned to dinner in Albany. — Fred tells me of a friend of his, Lady Lettice by name, who has slipped between the ferry and the quay at Piraeus while seeing off a friend, and fallen in the water. We both laugh; there was instant rescue; the image is funny and the reminder of Greece means – for Fred is a wily diplomat, knowing how to steer a conversation – that the question I asked of him will be answered soon, and that he still thinks of the trip we took together. 'I simply can't,' Fred says. We are holding balloons of brandy and sit opposite each other in this male bastion, as at that time Albany remained, like White's and the other gentlemen's clubs, the nest of Tories, squires, and right-wing journalists and politicians. (I make an exception for Fred: he is, as I tell myself, simply using Albany, where Guy Burgess would drunkenly stagger in to be cared for by him on too many late nights to go un-observed, availing himself of this arcaded, snobbish place as a cover for his true activities as third, fourth or fifth man.)

'I'm far too queer,' continues Fred, without a laugh this time but with a measure of enjoyment in his voice. In response I find I'm swirling the brandy – there are no balloon glasses at my parents' house, perhaps because the prospect of John McCubbin's cavalier waving of the slender-stemmed goblets brought too much anxiety to contemplate, so I am unused to the proper and manly way with them – and I notice to my displeasure that a large globule of the stuff has landed on my shirt. I spoil the drama and possible disappointment of the moment by dabbing like a distraught débutante at my lapel. — The moment passes and the matter is never referred to again, enabling several enjoyable trips – to Morocco, back to Greece and eventually to Laos when Fred is Ambassador there – to take place without any in-appropriate intentions on my part. — Fred's great weakness, as I was to learn the more I knew of him, was duchesses; and I believe he may have been tempted once or twice to marry a divorced or widowed duchess; but in the end, and to the delight of many, he married a charming woman and had children. I cannot say I felt, on leaving Albany that day, anything other than relief. — However, the problem of my future was yet again not solved.

EIGHT

Warhol Towers

Silhouette of Emma Tennant as Catherine Aydy,
author of *The Colour of Rain*
(by Elizabeth Glenconner)

Shoes – evening shoes, that is – are hard to find, at this time when the rich are still dressed in 'couture' and the poor struggle along dismal pavements with little but C&A or Richard Shops to sustain them. There were those who went to Charlotte Havelka and her kind, of course – and I remained loyal by force of habit, though the paper taffeta dress with sea green roses which received the contents of Noel Annan's coffee cup made me long for clothes that were disposable, or at least easy to clean. The occasion of the ruined taffeta took place at a grill in Knightsbridge, not far from the Normandie Hotel where Henry, Dig, their son and I had sat in gloomy silence all those years – or so it begins to seem – ago. My aunt, my mother's sister Anne, was present at the débâcle of the coffee cup, I think: she and her husband the philosopher Richard Wollheim were friends of the Annans and I can imagine no other reason for my presence there – the Provost Annan in an excited state upset the cup and the dress was forever marked, the espresso forming a black rose, sinister and alarming, on the thin silk. — Shoes, as I say, were even more difficult to arrive at. — I must have liked green, perhaps I thought it suited me: at Gamba in Dean Street in Soho I gave instructions for a pair of ballet pumps, low-heeled (I was tall; and at that time the worst humiliation was to be sent to a shop or shoe store specialising in Tall Girls, a fate I only narrowly avoided). At Gamba, probably before lunching at Chez Victor or going to the French pub to drink, I arranged for the dyeing of the white satin pumps. They will now be grass green, as if I have trudged through rained-on fields at a ball; they will match the green and white dress I intend to wear tonight, at a party where I may or may not meet someone. — But who can that person be, who would fit in with my strange cross-sexual tastes (not that these are put into practice: it's simply that the meeting of a young man I like is invariably accompanied by the wish to order identical outfits for him and me, suits of bright checks and colours, handsome, lad-like and, as would be said today, gay. — So I have slender hopes of coming across the twin brother I clearly crave. — My life as a fop (if such a term can be applied to a girl) is egged on by friends. — I am a snob, and famous, talented people are desirable to me: Cecil Beaton, who sees me tonight in the green and white dress (I draw his attention to my shoes, but this prime designer is unmoved by my brilliance); Douglas Cooper, who is an Australian collector of Picasso and Braque, sparring partner at the Tate where famously he attacked Sir John Rothenstein – who screams at me as I enter the drawing-room 'Nancy Cunard!' for, like most people, he thinks me rich and mad, like the poetic girl who was the first to publish Samuel Beckett. — I am drawn to elegance and beauty: Mark Boxer who first I saw shaking in a forest-green suit, on a barge on the Thames (the party tonight is in the house that is his and his wife Arabella's – she a queen of cookery writers who looks made of flour and butter and cream, as lightly baked as an American apple pie); the beautiful models who appear on the pages Mark designs, like greyhounds in a sea of lumpy women in dreary dresses; anyone and anything which will transport me from 'reality' – which consists of my need to find a new proper job (a falling out with the Boss at *Queen* and an unscheduled visit to Paris has led to my getting sacked). Any escape route from life at home, the food I slowly learn to cook, the knowledge of my inability to express myself as I so long to do, is enough to distract me now. As if in sympathy with my thwarted aims, fantastical houses and lovely vistas unravel before my eyes. I am asked to Mereworth, and find another rotunda, a Palladian building just like the Villa Malcontenta I visited with Chatwin, but this one in Kent, near Maidstone. John Betjeman is a guest there: he either wobbles or totters, intentionally it seems, along a gallery immensely long and furnished with birdcages and tattered-seated chairs and from the windows the Capability Brown landscape rises and falls, discreetly, far from industrial England which might as well never have existed at all. — In this world, where I seek the satisfaction I can never find, there is no history: only the present, which contains the finery of all previous epochs within it, like a museum of costume, furniture and painted heads.

It is 1962. I am back from New York, my first visit there; I am once more at Glen and about to write the novel without a name about the limited and self-concerned world which had for so long been mine. I understand the difference between England and America: the craving for fame and recognition of the inhabitants of one, the pretence of indifference (on the part of those known as the 'art and smart' at least) to such things in the country I know now I cannot leave. Watching the arrival of house martins at Glen (it must be late spring; the white daffodils are dying in the burn garden below the old kitchens and it is warm enough at last to go out without a heavy coat and gloves), I think of America: how I nearly escaped from England, the country where I feel constricted and restless – and how I have inevitably ended up here. I may be only twenty-four, but I must stay here for ever. I have a child; and not even the promise of a job in New York (the Features Department of American *Vogue*, shrine to the cult of the famous) has allowed me my wings. — Who will care for my son while I work? How far is Central Park, suitable for his outings, from the little apartment I was so pleased to find by myself? The whole plan was useless; I have returned to a blustery Boat Race, where my younger brother is rowing for Oxford; the shrill upper-class cries of spectators in the launch which accommodates family and friends; and the sense that this land of Ivy Compton-Burnett and John Betjeman will go on in the same way for as long as the island of Britain is surrounded by the sea. So it seems at the time – and I would certainly have made an effort to join the Angry Young Men if it hadn't been for the inconvenient fact of being a girl. There was little I could do but go north to Glen – still unaware of impending changes in the family structure, of my future expulsion from the Eden which keeps me breathing and happy even when I am in London, on one magazine or another.

I am sitting in the Oak Room, a room which in the past was allotted to my aunt Clare, and I am at a table not built to hold even a portable Olivetti typewriter, so frail are its legs under a polished rosewood top. I shall write – and it will be a novel which will be liked by Henry Green – or so I fervently hope. The cadences and affectations of the people of a world he has left behind; the strange poetry of London railway stations; the death of pigeons; the odd fleeting moments of lust and hopeless yearning which Henry portrays so unnervingly in his later novels (even if Evelyn Waugh described *Doting*, in a letter, as 'pitiful', it contains some feelings which Waugh never could convey) will of course not be captured by a novice writer like me. But the dialogue ('Don't use too many adverbs,' warns a friend of my mother's, James Pope-Hennessy, but I do. Without the mastery of Henry, it shows.) – the exchanges between the beehived young wives and the stuttering identical husbands – these I can surely portray. I have a good ear – or so I believe at least, for the editor Beatrix Miller, the first person to whom I showed a short story, has been kind to me. And another editor, Karl Miller at the *New Statesman*, has taken a book review: this proves, if only microscopically, that I can 'do' voices and prose, both.

I look back to London, and I dream of New York. The steam from the streets makes a fog of my thoughts: through a puff of grey and white smoke I see the long days, in my loaned apartment on the

Hudson, in my new identity (I am proclaimed as the daughter-in-law of Henry Green, and also as the niece of the philosopher Richard Wollheim). With these connections – and I soon discover connections are all-important in New York – I am saved from my reputation as Colin's sister – the tabloid fate, due to his friendship with Princess Margaret, which has helped to make me a figure of fun at home. I am taken into the heart of the intellectual life of America, at this time of Cold War and post-McCarthyism; I know the meaning of nothing but sit silent and entranced night after night as Philip Rahv and Dwight MacDonald and Bob Silvers and Eddy Morgan (voices of the *Paris Review* and the about-to-be-born *New York Review of Books*) argue and pronounce. In this world, too, is George Plimpton, with his romantic East River apartment, shabby and filled with books. — What am I (apart, of course, from Henry Green's daughter-in-law, etc.) to match the sang-froid and high spirits of Plimpton, with his casual WASP good looks and his determination to go out in the world – the world of professional boxing, of baseball or tennis or music, and prove he's no good at them at all? — How can I speak, when I know nothing and have so little to say? — But they are kind to me. The nights in Harlem, where Plimpton goes in for an amateur talent contest in the Apollo Theatre – at that time a place where cool Society people could go – suave Plimpton, with the blacks up above 121st Street one night, and with Jackie in the Colony Room the next.

'Order hundreds of red roses. Set them out all around you. Then I'll ring *Life* and you'll be photographed.' The speaker is Jeannie Campbell: her Scottish face, with its very white complexion, green eyes and frame of curly dark hair gives her a look of her then-husband, Norman Mailer. Jeannie embodies fame and high birth, in this most snobbish and insecure of cities, for she is also the granddaughter of the newspaper tycoon Lord Beaverbrook and the daughter of a Duke from the Highlands, the Duke of Argyll. Jeannie is a friend of my half-brother Colin.

'Why should I?' I say. There is something in Jeannie that makes me think of Colin's 'Well done!' as I opened the Ball with an ill-executed foxtrot; what had I done?

'You'll be famous,' Jeannie says in a tone which suggests I am sillier than she thought. 'Everyone will want to ask you to their parties.'

But I am happy with the world into which my purloined identity has plunged me. I am here and loving my time here precisely because I am not in 'Society' – not that this prevents me from taking up the invitation of a lost, disaffected woman I have met in London, wife of a millionaire, who has offered me for free the use of the company apartment at the very top of the Waldorf Towers. There, as is said of me by those who wish to mock me in England, I can 'have my grouse and eat it': I can be bohemian, literary and still thirty-odd floors up in the most expensive building in New York. — 'Go on, *do* get the roses,' Jeannie insists, still to no avail. She is after all married to the author of *Advertisements for Myself*.

In my tower there are, unsurprisingly, many parties and invited and uninvited guests. Mailer comes and sits for hours, clearly hoping for an orgy, which fails to take place. I am visited in the Waldorf Towers by my friend David Winn, the tallest and funniest of the group who, along with the actor Peter Eyre and my now-resident-at-8-Cheyne-Walk-friend Christopher Gibbs make me laugh in London between ill-starred forays into romance. Winn comes to stay in the Waldorf Towers. Marguerite Lamkin who taught Elizabeth Taylor to speak Southern in the movie *Giant* introduces me to Andy Warhol. — He is drawing feet still and shoes for glossy magazines; but his first Campbell's soup can appears and Winn somehow gets it. (Was he given it, did he steal it? Like the marble bottom at the Villa Malcontenta, it just turns up one day.) David Winn's laugh – he was drowned in a dreadful accident less than eighteen months later, with his girlfriend, sailing in Sandwich Bay – lasts over the years, as do the memories of his high amusement at the luxury and pretensions of the tower where I had landed soon after arriving in New York; and his instant love for Americans (he was himself descended from one of Nancy Astor's sisters), to many of whom – or so it seemed at the time – he was the perfect representation of a witty, idio-syncratic Englishman. Then, Marguerite takes me to see Claes Oldenburg's sculptures at their initial showing in 1st Street: the plaster wedding dress so corny and over-copied now, so strange and original at the time.

'Get them all photographed,' Marguerite says; we are on our way to the Peppermint Lounge, where the music and the stunning girls dancing high on a bar are intoxicating to anyone trained to mooch around marquees at country balls to the sad imitations of

Ambrose and his Band. 'Sell them to your magazine!
Give them to *Queen*, for heaven's sake!' Marguerite's
Louisiana drawl, her collapsible smile and her pointy
chin are right up close to me. She suggests a
photographer, Frederick Eberstadt. I agree: no one in
England has heard of this new explosion of Pop Art,
as it is known, in New York; besides, I would rather
organise the photographing of a papier mâché bride
than pose myself, engulfed in red roses. — We dance;
we sit up late with Emil de Antonio, known as 'Dee',
who tells me he was married to Gloria Vanderbilt
and one day he simply 'got out of the car at the lights'
and they never met again. Dee is a philosopher and so
far into the avant-garde that he may fall off the edge:
he is making his documentary on the McCarthy
hearings; later, when the real Sixties come and claim
him, he will produce a movie of a man sleeping for
twenty-four hours, a movie twenty-four hours long.
Dee sees the wit and originality in my friend David
Winn, and I believe he may have been responsible for
procuring the Warhol soup can for Winn, but both
are dead now and there is no way of finding out.

All the time I'm in New York I sense the coming
failure of my plan to stay there; and I act, like a girl
given the part of a girl to play, as if a new man, a new
life will make it possible for me to feel the freedom of
America (although of course I have no idea of how
miserable and constricted I would be if I found myself
trapped in any world other than the highly international world of intellectuals my spurious connections have produced for me). An instinct, and
probably a certain amount of common sense, propels
me towards the suitable (and glamorous – they must

be that) Nelson Aldrich, handsome son of a distinguished and celebrated family. I stay at his grandmother's house in Boston: I see myself from outside as girls are prone to do, as I walk through yellowing snowdrifts, 'discussing' politics and literature with Nelson (I understand very little of what he says). Yet I feel the melancholy of the mansion house and the unmelting snow and the aged grandmother with her Irish maids and I flee back to New York – for isn't melancholy exactly what I am trying to escape? — I stay with Peter Duchin at Carnegie Hall, in a studio where the strains from practising musicians sound day and night: now I am in an Antonioni movie and float, more self-conscious than even I have ever been, around the great bare space while the son of the pianist Eddie Duchin and Kim Novak, dark and good-looking, sings and plays the piano. It is all too good to be true – and indeed so it turns out to be, for there is no depth in any of my feelings. I am playing out a girl lost in New York; and in any case I see Duchin's features darken with disbelief and suspicion when, on slicing a grapefruit in two for our breakfast together, I cut it the wrong way. Instead of segments a blank expanse of yellow-green looks up from the kitchen board. 'You mean you don't even know how to cut a *grapefruit* in half?' my host demands. — Most important, I am at all times unable to make up my mind. One fascinating American seems as alluring as the next. Even as I am offered the job on American *Vogue* and find the little apartment for myself and my son, I know none of this is really going to happen. — Before I know it, two and a half months have passed, and it's time to go home – to the flat at 8 Cheyne Walk, to the static and dreary (or so it appeared then) world of men in Old Etonian ties and talk about Cyril Connolly. A letter from Jacob Rothschild, to my surprise, informs me we can no longer meet due to his forthcoming marriage. As I stare at the letter, wondering if it's a duplicate, I hear that *Queen* magazine turned down the scoop of Warhol and Oldenburg's work as 'too boring'. It is time for things to change.

NINE

I Married a Satirist

Osbert Lancaster's jacket illustration for
The Colour of Rain

For a girl to seem 'different', as was generally accepted at that time, a change of hair-style – or, more drastically, a change of hair colour as well as style – was final proof of a seismic alteration in personality, ambitions or love object. In my case, the simple desire for change is expressed in my black hair, short but fiercely fringed, and the corresponding oddness of my complexion and clothes. 'It doesn't . . . it doesn't really . . .' begins my mother, trying as always to be tactful when faced with my monstrous transmogrifications, most of which, like my permanent emigration to the United States, turn out to come to very little in the end. But I stick it out, an over-large Audrey Hepburn verging on Anna Magnani: yet again I am so unsure of who I am that I don't even know who I'm trying to look like. — On occasion, inspired by the fact I have written – in ten days – my novel about the vacuous young couples of Kensington, I put on a beret and stare anxiously at my reflection in the Chinese Chippendale mirror procured for me by Christopher Gibbs. I am a writer – the publishing firm of Weidenfeld & Nicolson has taken my book – but the beret sits awkwardly on my black-dyed hair and when I walk down the King's Road I receive as many inimical or puzzled looks – or so I imagine – as the odd person of Chelsea, Quentin Crisp (to be seen in the King's Road or Fulham Road sometimes, pursued by jeering boys). — My changed appearance doesn't of course lead to attacks on my person; but, as I stagger from the Eaton Square flat of one set of friends to the little house in Trevor Square in Knightsbridge, to see Francis and his mother Violet Wyndham, I make secret plans to apply a coat of yellow dye and return to my old self. — No such dye, as spiteful friends are pleased to tell me, actually exists. So I must discuss the fortunes of my book, due to be published in the spring, with a head of lustreless jet-black hair. As I approach friends' houses I remove the beret, but I never sink so low as to don a scarf.

My book, which is very short and almost entirely in dialogue, will be sent to Henry Green. I have found the title *The Colour of Rain* in Paris, in the rue du Bac apartment, not with the charming villain/hero of my novel, Evvy as I have named him, but with a young pianist Michel Bloch, who rests his finger along with mine on an upturned glass and asks the planchette for guidance. — The novel is about nothing; when the glass nudges letters on the table which spell out *la couleur de la pluie*, it seems accurate and even poetic; finding my *nom de plume* (for I cannot write as Emma Yorke, I hardly have the temerity to call myself Green; and my own patronym will shortly belong to my younger brother's wife: she will be Emma Tennant and may not wish to stand accused of having authored *The Colour of Rain*) is more challenging. My name is determined less successfully by the spirits and I shall be Catherine Aydy. — Well satisfied, we cease playing the planchette – though I was to wish, later, thinking of that particular episode, that I had asked the supernatural powers what the fate of my book would be.

Bruce Chatwin comes to England, his face clear

and hair the enviable sunshine hue I must wait an age for, until the ugly black roots have died out. He and I go to a house I have been lent by a friend for a weekend in the country – actually and perhaps unfortunately in a village named Great Bedwyn – the house comfortable and grand, disguised as a cottage and heavily staffed with excellent cook and maids, the double bed into which Chatwin and I retire after dinner so soft and deeply decked with Irish linen of an irreproachable whiteness that neither of us can move. (Though this may not, of course, have been the sole reason.) On return from such adventures I invariably go to Trevor Square, to the charming little eighteenth-century house Henry Green claimed he could see into from his upstairs lavatory. I greet Violet in her sitting-room, and I later go up to Francis's sitting-room and he tells me of the books he has read and the writers he has discovered, among them Jean Rhys, long thought by the literary world to be dead (but he has kept in touch with her and now she is found to be alive: with his encouragement in the depths of her obscurity and poverty, she will write *Wide Sargasso Sea*). I think of a past inhabitant of this house, Harriet Wilson, the courtesan – of his entry in whose memoirs the Duke of Wellington famously pronounced 'Publish and be Damned'. My own representation of the follies and vanities of the rich and high-born in the London of the early 1960s will not merit an equal degree of outrage or attention – though, as I shall discover, those who dislike the way they are portrayed will no longer invite me or wish to chat on the phone. I find I have, inadvertently, written my own version of *Hurting*, and

Henry, though he sends me an enthusiastic letter on the subject of *The Colour of Rain*, is less kind in person when I visit him in the large house in Wilton Place to which he and Dig moved at the time of their son's marriage. Here, Henry wears mittens against the cold in his half-landing room which smells of gin. He watches sport on TV; apart from a glancing remark to the effect that I haven't really 'brought it off', he fails to divulge any opinions or secrets of his own mastery of the craft.

'Are you *ready*?' — Elaine Dundy is American, married to the revered theatre critic Ken Tynan (although I don't know her for that but for *The Dud Avocado*, her novel of an American girl in Paris which is funny and touching and true). Elaine has a black-and-white check tweed jacket: I see her very bright against a rainy London window; she brings to this country a touch of prickliness, of the disrespect we have all become used to doing without, loyal as we are to Queen, Government and any other institution which commands patriotic obedience. Are we ready – for this small, pixie-looking woman whose wit, knowledge of American movies, American writing, American everything brings an intoxicating sense of freedom? Whether we are ready or not, Elaine brings the promise of something new, the suggestion that, magically, anything she thinks possible will and can take place. It is no surprise, therefore, that she is the first to hear of the new satire that will, as she proclaims, sweep the country and sweep away as well the aroma of over-ripe pheasant and port, the diet of upper-class politicians as corrupt as the statesmen of the *ancien régime*, and restore scorn and sarcasm to their rightful place in the English psyche. Elaine has met these new young satirists. She will take me to be a part of a studio audience for *That Was The Week That Was,* a TV programme which infuriates and excites the British public. And I, intrigued right through the summer by the extraordinary happenings in the Profumo case, go with her, the perfect companion and guide to the new wave of disrespect which has come at last to our shores. At this event – or after the filming of sketches which seem to me brilliantly original and scathing of the present Government – though a few are heard to remark tartly that this is schoolboy stuff or, at their best, on the level of Cambridge *Footlights* – I shall meet those responsible for this swingeing (a good new word) satire on our rulers (though not on the monarchy except in the feeblest sense. Some things are sacred, after all.). Elaine, iridescent in the dogtooth tweed, fades into the background when the show is over. — I have met a satirist and I decide then and there to ally myself to this new movement: isn't he one of the band behind the new satirical magazine *Private Eye*? I don't see myself as a target but as a contributor. — There is even a club in Soho called the Establishment where I shall go night after night and on occasion see Lenny Bruce, worshipped – and rightly – by the young men who now appear school-boys in comparison with him. — But I am as blind to this at the time as any star-struck teenager, waiting for the pop star at the stage door. I am a part of this scintillating, dangerous new world. Elaine comes with me or visits 8 Cheyne Walk where Luisa serves great platters of spaghetti carbonara to those who

157

mock all the older generation venerates and loves: heroes of the First World War; Bloomsbury in the shape of Lytton Strachey and Virginia Woolf; religion and romantic love. There is nothing that stands unreviled, at the end of the room overlooking the river at 8 Cheyne Walk. Bernard Levin speaks beguilingly; red wine is put down on the table with a thud by Luisa (it has been as much as I can do to keep away John McCubbin, for I would certainly have appeared in *Private Eye* if a butler had been present; John, however, would have found something to laugh about; he might never, in the relative sobriety of my parents' house, have enjoyed himself in quite the same way again). The world was at the feet of this group – it never occurred to me that they were, with the exception of the singer Millicent Martin, all male – and they were much in demand, the single of Harold Macmillan croaking his 'Winds of Change' speech to a musical background becoming a smash hit in that summer of Cliveden, Stephen Ward and the much castigated Christine Keeler. There seems to be no end to the satire, and no way the Government can ever be looked at seriously again. I am proud to be a part of this sudden, unblinking stare at reality – the reality of secrets and lies, their cover-up and the meek acceptance on the part of the public of the veils drawn over anything that might cause trouble.

By proxy, I am a satirist myself. In April, in the spring after the exciting winter of *That Was The Week*, I marry again, to Christopher Booker, who is bespectacled as all good satirists should be, at Chelsea Register Office. Unfortunately, I choose to practise my new 'satirical' voice on the registrar and produce a parody of the marriage service. My new mother-in-law, a long cry from the subtle and delightful Dig, and deeply religious, cannot have liked my performance; but – perhaps unluckily – the clerk decides to pay no attention to my tiresomely silly rendering of the words and pronounces us man and wife. My hair is still black and I wear a daffodil in my brown suede coat. Afterwards, at my parents' house in Swan Walk, there is a large reception. My mother and father are both relieved that I have found someone at last; but my son, who dislikes the whole performance as much as I am about to do, refuses to take this union to heart. Despite bribes and coaching, 'Mr Booker' is how my new satirist husband is addressed by this obdurate five-year-old. We go away after the wedding party and come back to find 'Mr Booker' has been sacked behind his back from the board of *Private Eye*. This is the first intimation of the loyalty and friendship to be expected from satirists and comes as a blow. 'Are you ready?' exclaims Elaine when she is told of these nefarious goings-on. Certainly I was not; and there is the question, for the new autocrat of the Cheyne Walk breakfast table, of finding a job, and soon.

In the midst of all this, the proofs of my novel arrive. I take them to the Ritz; it is a freezing winter and I can't stand another night in my unheated flat. Somehow I have smuggled in a girl, a cousin and friend who also lacks any heating in her flat; she sleeps on the floor, on a mattress. — I have no idea how I organised this in the Ritz – but I did. As ever, the sense of excitement provoked by even the mildest cause for celebration (in this case the appearance of *The Colour of Rain* in a mock-up of its purple and green jacket with the Osbert Lancaster drawing of nannies and young mothers in beehives and checked suits pushing prams) leads me to spend every penny I have. — In point of fact I have very little to celebrate. Paul and Ingrid Channon, depicted in the novel as a couple who had married almost by mistake (in fact they were devoted to each other and were right to complain) don't like the book at all. I've heard that other characters meet to discuss their grievances. The services of a lawyer are engaged; and, at the time of my standing at the window on the first floor of the Ritz, looking out at the grey freeze-up of Piccadilly traffic, the women in black mink coats stepping from cars and into Fortnum and Mason, and the top of a red bus as it goes slowly past, I have just returned from my meeting with the lawyer and agreed to change Channon's redbrick late Georgian house in Essex into a Gothic pile, and water down some of the sillier jokes made by his predecessor, Jonathan Guinness. — For all the possible disaster involved in the publication of the book – the lawyer has looked grave and hinted at injunctions – I feel an important writer. And the fact that Barley Alison, the editor, has suggested putting the book in for the Prix Formentor makes me all the more pleased with myself. My mother has executed a silhouette of an enigmatic figure – Catherine Aydy, the author – and this will be on the inside back jacket. I am pseudonymous – just like Henry Green.

The next intimations that all is not well with the fortunes of this slender volume appear a couple of months later, at 8 Cheyne Walk. The blossom is at its peak in the streets of Chelsea and my black hair is finally growing out, leaving a mottled effect which is now disguised by the then-fashionable 'streaks'. More like a brindled cat than I had wished, I am nevertheless cock-a-hoop: I have been to New York with Mr Booker; we have gone on down to the Caribbean, to see the island Colin has exchanged for the unwanted Trinidad estate; and the fact that we have almost nothing in common (Mr Booker and I, that is) and nothing to say to each other has been masked by our pleasant reception in America: lunches and drinks and a party given for us by the endlessly hospitable George Plimpton. We are artists, and I am finally grown up; we are a novelist and a satirist; though we might have done better to exchange professions there and then, as neither manifestation of our talents appears to go on to success or financial reward. — News comes in gradually of the dinner parties given by the slighted characters in my novel; it is said of one of them that a copy of the book, with a cast list of the originals pinned to the flyleaf, is taken out by her at dinner to general laughter. The Prix Formentor is said to have been a fiasco; Quentin Crewe, an erstwhile colleague at *Queen*, reports that the chairman of the judges, Alberto Moravia, tossed the novel into a waste-basket, and went on to condemn it as symptomatic of the decadence in Britain. The sense of success enjoyed in the city of Jeannie Campbell and Andy Warhol shows itself as false and evaporates fast. I want to be a serious writer yet people say, when they see me coming towards them, 'Nancy Mitford' (whose novels, as I would now be the first to admit, are infinitely more accomplished than *The Colour of Rain*). All I knew then, with the accusations of being either Cunard or Mitford, poor-little-rich, would-be bohemian or portraitist of a dotty, cold-hearted upper class, was that I couldn't, or so it appeared, escape my fate: I was a Nancy.

The summer is coming, and I decide we must go to a Greek island. 'The trouble with you,' says Judy, over from the Isola Tiberina and avid for balls, gossip, impending break-ups and unsuitable matches, 'is that you're an orgiast. You want too much all at the same time.' And it's true I do want to make my lack of feeling for anyone into a patchwork of old feelings: Fred shall be represented by the white house on the island, Hydra, which I shall rent from an elderly couple of Jamesian charm who live in Athens, and whose name is Sedgwick; past days at country houses, in Kent or Wiltshire, and the memory of fleeting infatuations will provide the picnics and house parties I am determined to hold there (the house turns out to be far too small, in the event, for such grandiose plans: there is just room for my son, the au pair and ourselves). Before all this, however, comes the first stirring of changes in the family: changes which, despite my only too evident girlitude, will have a far-reaching effect.

TEN

Lenin's Tomb

Christopher Booker in Greece, 1964

I am standing by a piano in a hotel somewhere on the south coast. 'Mr Booker' is there, but the focus is bad and I can't see him clearly. My son and I have been deep-sea fishing – but with whom or how I don't know. I do know, as I hold the receiver and a waiter comes into the dingy, deserted ballroom where I have taken the call, that the subject of the call is the house I have put in a bid for. I am told the bid was successful: I can now leave the flat at 8 Cheyne Walk, with its running-down lease and lack of garden, and move down the road. — My new house has a room almost the size of this one, but it's more of a studio – next to the house where J. M. W. Turner lived and painted the river. How have I got this house? The family business, so I have heard, is in the process of being sold. I have no shares in C. Tennant Sons, unlike the men in the family. Somehow, however, my father has seen that I am able to buy a house. Before I move there, of course, I must dispose of the flat.

Something tells me I shall move from 8 Cheyne Walk – which, infected by the atmosphere of money that has come suddenly into every conversation, I have had decorated by the fashionable interior designer David Hicks – without 'Mr Booker'. 'Why did you leave him behind in the flat?' a friend asks, when exactly this comes to pass. 'In that Lenin's tomb?' (He refers to the bed, not a four-poster but with an overhead 'tester' as it is known, all covered in scarlet fabric: both an expensive and a pretentious reminder of such beds in grand country houses and, as my friend enjoys pointing out, singularly ill-suited, in its Bolshevik appearance, to the views and politics of the man I have married at leisure and repent in haste.) — It has become increasingly clear, as the months and seasons pass, that satirists are really *Telegraph* readers in disguise: like schoolboys in a private school, they have a bullying tone when attacking others that is not far from 'Disgusted of Tunbridge Wells', their magazine similar to the rag which the children of Disgusted produce in the holidays to stave off boredom at a shortage of further victims to bully. – My friends, in their rotundas, in London houses or simply in the country without any grudge against anyone, have been surprised by the satirists' love of butlers; and less than pleased when their own homes are described in newspaper articles. Now I feel the despair and emptiness another wrong decision has cost me and I know the reason for my foolish extravagance with the flat. I have little taste for the ornate William Morris chrysanthemums, the Chinese yellow gloss and the thick curtains with which I have swathed my once-ordinary and likeable home and cannot help the guilt and confusion I feel at my obvious – but unspoken – intention to do just as my friend prophesied. I shall leave 'Mr Booker' – but I don't know yet for whom.

Now the viewfinder, the recorder of those sudden, brightly lit scenes which furnish memory, moves from the ill-furnished south coast hotel, with its late-afternoon sadness and smell of potted shrimp teas and wet gym shoes. It swings, first into the darkness of a Greek night, where stars give all the light needed for two people, a beautiful young man and a girl I know, to come up a path and knock on a door set in a high whitewashed wall. It waits, this patient lens, until the moon is fully out. Then, with a child already tucked up in bed and a bespectacled man frowning out to sea as if praying for deliverance, we come in on another girl – it is myself. It settles finally for a close-up on the features of the beautiful young man. He is younger than I am, and walking beside me on the dried-out earth of the grove. — Then the black cloth comes down and the night goes on as it always has, on the island of Hydra where there are no cars and only a donkey walks stiffly up the white-painted steps, brushing against us as we run down to music, to the disco that lies under trees, in the hot night air by the port.

Luc is the name of the beautiful young man and the girl he has come with I have known since we were children; the most agreeable of girls – sharp-witted but apparently perfectly content with the new arrangement, which will be a trip round Greece, the southern Peloponnese this time, ending in the Mani where I, dying of love already, am indeed happy to end up for the rest of my life. This girl, so unlike me, benevolently smiling on the romance that grows under her nose, makes it possible for the journey to take place. — Mr Booker, I believe, either saw nothing or came along for no other reason than it was something to do: Lenin's tomb can't have seemed

167

inviting at the height of summer. He neither smiles nor frowns as we drive the length of Greece in baking heat and sleep afternoons into evenings as sudden as the shadow of the pines when they lengthen across the interminable road. — The summer will never end; yet already everything I see or hear is filled with this sense of an ending: a train hoots, across the wide plains of Kalamata, and I foresee (accurately as it turns out) the end of our love – on Luc's part of course, not mine. (In all true romances the heroine must die, or at least be left.) — At night we go up into the hills; we must have air; we gasp in the plateia where a tree, lit up by the lights of the taverna, drops wizened olives into our glasses. I am escaping, properly, at last. — As it turns out, my sense of a writing of last words proves, also, true: back at Glen and reunited with my son and parents I feel the first tremors of the quake that will lift them from the homes I expect them to remain in all their lives. Children, or at least girls, fear the departure or loss of a mother and father to care for their own children when it is necessary. What will become of me, if I actually have to look after my life, my responsibilities, all by myself?

None of this prevents me from continuing on the escape route as if I hadn't a care in the world. — The world is where I will live. — I am thinking of ordering identical tartan silk suits for myself and Luc: will the shop up in Elgin supply the material? Which tartan shall it be? For Luc has Scottish blood along with a mix of exciting descents, he is a plaid all to himself and I draw out a design: we shall have our very own. — The whimsy and impracticality of my life become more pronounced and my mother looks sad. — At dinner at Glen, I outline my plan for Italy followed by an autumn in Paris where Luc will improve his French (for what? My poor mother looks as if she thinks it must be in order to pass an exam, for she has heard of the unsuitability of this youth). It goes without saying, my son will come too, and the current Australian au pair, who jumps at the chance. — I do not consider, unsurprisingly, the reaction of anyone else; and when my son's father appears in the apartment I have rented in the Boulevard Montparnasse, next door to the Closerie des Lilas where I sit on a high stool and sip crème de menthe on crushed ice, staring at my reflection next to Samuel Beckett's in the art nouveau glass behind the bar, I am astonished when he declares the apartment 'not a real home' and threatens to take my son away. — The stalls laden with oysters and *oursins*, the long walks down the rue Vaugirard, the Luxembourg Gardens and the trudges round the Louvre must now all come to an end. But not before I realise my greatest ambition, which is to experience the tragedy of my greatest hero at first hand. — On my twenty-seventh birthday I go with Luc to the Hôtel d'Alsace off the Boulevard St-Germain (a hotel now made smart and lacking in the 'atmosphere' my melo-dramatic nature demanded at that time). In the little suite of rooms where Oscar Wilde spent his last weeks I walk, sit and dream, on red velvet-upholstered chairs in the tiny sitting-room, or in the bedroom where it's just possible to squeeze round the end of the bed because the management have seen fit to put in a low wall, a bidet and a bath along the far end of the room. But the battered table he must have used to write on is there; and a fig tree in the dark little courtyard beyond the window. Here is the wallpaper of which Oscar remarked that either he or it would have to go. He it was who went; though I don't believe the vomit-coloured paper, witness to my birthday over sixty years after the death of Wilde, could actually have been the same as the murderous original.

My new house in London is let to an American businessman while we are away in Paris. He is cooked and cleaned for by Luisa, who tells hair-raising stories when we return of his naked rush to the lavatory in the morning and his yelling command that a succession of neat whiskies be brought to him as he sits there. — Luisa has enjoyed herself in the role of chatelaine of 118 Cheyne Walk (as this house is, with a back door through a garden into Apollo Place) but she is glad to have me back again. She wants to wake us in the morning as we sleep on the platform above the studio (painted white, it resembles more and more an empty swimming pool). She likes to lower a tray of coffee and a huge number of chipolata sausages on to the prone form of a beautiful young man. — But reality is beginning to creep too close for my liking. I have to take a job – at *Vogue* this time, in the Features Department where I must interview artists and those who like to spend money and buy the work of artists. I have to learn to flatter those who are rich and self-satisfied, in print; and soon, despite the kindness of editor and colleagues, I leave. Luc begins to travel, going, as it seems to me, further and further, and returning too tired from

Brasilia or Peru to remember where he lives. — It is plain for all to see that he will go for good one day soon and I will be left dreaming of the life in Paris before we were pulled back: of the room that was long and wood-floored overlooking the Boulevard Montparnasse: the kitchen with cockroaches (these I never minded, but they were considered a sign of how beyond control our little ménage had become); of trips to the Musée Carnavalet where the last days of the ill-fated King of France are laid out in his journal, under glass in spidery writing, recording 'Rien'. Nothing in London, in this narrow house that is so noisy in front where the traffic on the Embankment thunders past and so sepulchrally quiet at the back, can match the excitement and glamour of the existence I had made for us in Paris. — I stand in the big room at 118 Cheyne Walk, wondering how I will earn and what I will do. And my parents come one evening to find me there dancing alone: I am proud of my new dress, pink as the rules of girlitude could desire, plain on top, then flaring into a great patterned skirt of pinks and reds. Where does the narcissism come from? My uncle Stephen possibly – but even I am wary of blaming my grandmother Pamela's 'jewels' for fear of ending as a true amalgam of them all.

On the occasion of this visit, my father is (very unusually for him) emotional and distraught and at last I stop the music, *La Traviata* (he doesn't care much for music anyway, and my girlish dancing must have been maddening to him then). My mother looks as if she would prefer the twirling to go on. — My son runs in. — My father kisses him. — Then he says

– how do I know then that something changes? I can't tell what – he says, 'We *are* close as a family, aren't we?'

This is the first time my father has spoken to me like this and I know it has to do with the sale of the family business, with the changes in my parents' lives I don't want to see. — I nod, and say yes, knowing my answer is a feeble one. — Then, embarrassed, I run to put the music on; my father sits miserably there until 'Sempre Libera' has ended (the song of Violetta's freedom which reflects, surely, my sense of imprisonment: but what I was imprisoned by and what my actual freedom would have consisted of, it would have been impossible to say).

What went wrong? I stagger from crisis to crisis – there is never enough money and Luc becomes increasingly distant. We move from room to room in the house as if we are engaged in forming a language map of the world: high in the front above the traffic we are dazzled by a gold-yellow river glinting in the early morning, driving us to rise; in the studio, behind the galleried area where Luisa likes to catch us, we sleep in a room like an Eskimo's hut, so low and round-windowed we struggle to stay awake. Wherever we find ourselves, it is impossible to communicate. My son and the au pair move when we do, the house a constantly changing landscape of chests of drawers, old sofas, odds and ends from my flat at 8 Cheyne Walk, vacated for good now by the second man I had married by accident. There is no peace here. — You learn the hard way, says Luisa, laughing, for she knows every detail of our lives, however much we may try to keep them from her.

At Glen, doors close and I know my timing to be excruciating, always a sign of unhappiness, of misjudgment in love. — No one had told me the house where I had spent my childhood is this very week being made over to Colin; perhaps my father's agitation can be traced to this, but I will never know. My son and I are alone in the house I no longer feel is haunted by the ghosts of the family: I have too many ghosts of my own by now to care about the faded disappointments of my grandmother, her white dresses, her white vellum-bound books.— My sister-in-law shows us we aren't welcome; this, though, a sharp reminder of my great-aunt Margot and her own sister-in-law, my grandmother Pamela: 'Sisters-in-law just don't get on,' my father said firmly to me when I exclaimed in surprise at feelings expressed on those family occasions when such relationships are brought into the light. — We have to leave, my son and I. — The dark night road, bordered with rough heather and grass, lies in the headlamps of the car, driven by Tommy, from Glen – Tommy who can be counted on to laugh when he remembers his story of John McCubbin and the 'rotten' door of the car he went to Galashiels in, to collect my father from the train. Neither of us speaks, for all the thirty-eight miles to Edinburgh and Waverley Station. — That night I dream again, of my father and of my son, and then of my son and my brother and sister-in-law's son Henry, who stays behind in the house with them, wondering why we have gone.

Back in London, I read and try to write in the 'studio' at the long trestle table I bought in Pimlico Road, in a shop made for suckers like me: 'The top is much older than the base,' says Gibbs. 'You paid too much; but it's a friendly old table' (disheartening words if ever I heard them). Poor David Winn is dead and his Warhol soup can hangs on the ugly, ill-proportioned wall with the gallery high above it, looking the size of a postage stamp there: his mother has decided I should inherit it. But the sight of the can, reminding me of Winn and the laughs we had with Dee in New York, makes me sad and I go to Robert Fraser's gallery and exchange it for a water-colour of a collapsing sofa. 'Are you going to have that made?' my father asks politely, thinking it a plan for a seating area: whatever it is, this work by Colin Self is certainly one of the worst swaps for a Warhol I could have brought off. — I dream of Paris, already long forgotten by Luc, and of the white crystal, perfectly formed like a flower from a distant planet, a rose or a tulip petrified in a magical glacier, glowing with the pink light behind it, that was in a little shop in the rue de Seine. I loved the crystal, which was too expensive to buy, and I wish now I had got it somehow, like Chatwin and the marble bottom: there are some things that are lucky to have and you regret their loss without ever having had them. — But this of course was a way of thinking that my association with Luc – and with the people who surrounded us – made easy. We listened to songs by Jacques Brel and Charles Aznavour and queued at the NFT: these were the early days of the mania for old films and a friend, Jon Halliday, wrote a book on the secret Marxist message of Douglas Sirk, technicolored *auteur* of *All That Heaven Allows*. My son listened to the Beatles – and I did too, when I wanted to feel cheerful.

What more did I want, now I had Luc, my Olivetti portable at the long table, and friends to supper? I cooked them mutton dishes from the pages of Elizabeth David and threw in cognac at the last moment, in despair. (My friend Jane Miller, writer and teacher, told me of her stint in Cambridge, Mass. with her husband Karl, and of a supper visit from Edmund Wilson; of a duck which refused to cook, and finally, falling on the fluffy carpet, had to be hacked into small pieces and served up: 'What's it called?' one of the guests had asked, and Jane laughs as she tells it, throwing back her head and then pulling a small cigar from the depths of her black bag.) — Sometimes Luisa came, and in an impossibly short time there appeared a perfect ring of spinach; osso buco and rice and oranges sliced thin, in a sugary juice. — But Luisa needs money, lots of money. I don't have it. My knuckles of mutton and cheap stews come in huge cast-iron pots and Luc stays out, 'working' – something to do with photography or film; it is never really convincing or clear.

The studio looks out the back on a paved, un-appealing garden. There is a side door, and from Apollo Place, from the little house the suicided painter Johnny Minton left her, comes Henrietta Moraes. She has recently broken a leg and is on velvet-covered crutches; her eyes are wild. Henrietta, who has been the torch of Soho, who has performed her fandango in York Minster and has been painted again and again by Francis Bacon, and who is a friend of my friend and cousin Francis, who has always defended and loved her: Henrietta waves a crutch at the ill-made french windows that open on

175

to our patch of stone and dead grass, and demands to be let in. She is drunk and on drugs – and so is everyone beginning to be, in this world where the first shadows of the future are falling – but, although I drink a good deal I know my drug to be beauty, an indefinable gift possessed by Luc and existing in the places, pictures and buildings he leads me to. — I believe, at that time, I would have understood the need to sacrifice everything to beauty, to go from remote shore to austere mountain to capture and preserve it; and then, when it becomes clear that these places remain beautiful while their worshippers grow old and vile, let go and die. — This was nonsense, and I knew it. A romantic dream: it filled the void created by the lack of the family I wanted, the perfectly middle-class security I often craved. — For these were not, in the company I kept, likely to be provided for me. And at that time it would have been thought impossible for a girl to imagine providing them for herself.

The desire for beauty, and the need to attract my dreamy lover with my own beautiful sites, takes me to a number of places in the summer of 1966, the first being the Woodford Valley in Wiltshire, where the River Avon runs between banks of an enamelled green and the house built by my grandfather for Pamela, my beauty-seeking grandmother, is poised on a lawn just above the river: grey-stone, mullioned windows looking out on bulrushes, yellow flag iris

and a boathouse crouched by the water's edge. — I
find a cottage there, empty and fitted out with wide
doors and baths, and all the comforts my poor father
thinks are needed by his eccentric, once flamboyant
brother, Stephen, now the near-bankrupt occupant
of the manor house at Wilsford. — But Stephen has
refused to go there. The old village green by the side
of the house – 'old' indeed by the time I stand at
Wilsford and look through the trunks of beeches, like
everything else in this over-beautified landscape
reminiscent of a Walter Crane illustration to a fairy
tale, disproportionately large and unreal in appearance – was made by Pamela. A bungalow, the last
type of building she would have wanted amongst her
simulated dovecotes and make-believe barns, has
been placed amongst the tree trunks. Dwarfed by the
sheer size of the beeches, dark in winter and summer
alike, the bungalow has as tenants the writer V. S.
Naipaul and his wife Pat. They have become friends
with my father and mother; and, slightly apprehensively, live in the shadow of my uncle, who now
seldom leaves the house and so they never meet. —
But when I go to Wilsford with Luc, I am allowed in
by the back door and stare through an open glass
door to the Florida stage set Stephen has made,
perhaps in my grandmother's memory (if Pamela had
lived longer, America, rather than a replica of a
Thomas Hardy green, might have been her choice of
landscape), and we see Stephen, long-haired, rumi-
native among the stone flamingos and giant cowrie
shells which litter the sheltered front of the house. —
I ask Louis Ford, who cares for my uncle, if I can buy
a watercolour – and I do, for £25. It has the pinks and

magentas my uncle favours, these swirling about the torsos of sailors in the port at Marseilles. — But, instead of admiration in Luc's face I see amusement and scorn. — I know my family always to have bought beauty – whether at Glen, in the hills of southern Scotland, or down here, in a lush country where the river forms channels in the meadows across from the house, bright strips of tinsel there in winter and great swathes of buttercups in the heat of May and June. — I am miserably aware that my uncle is the only member of the family who could be described as an 'artist'. Luc and his family and friends are the real thing: they make beauty (his mother sculpts and is known); and they find beauty – but they don't need to buy it. — For all the shame I may feel, the view of the river and the long, softly green and yellow meadows on the far side of the water where my son fishes by the swampy bottom of my new garden, is extraordinarily beautiful. Luc and I don't stay there long, however: there is always a good reason to be on the move.

The pursuit of beauty blinds the pursuer, as is well known, to the truth; and in this year of the temporary (even the cottage on the banks of the River Avon cannot be mine for long: it is part of what is left of my uncle's estate, a dwindling couple of fields and a stable block behind the house which estate agents, anxious for a profit, are doing up for no known future resident), the truth is hard to find. Shall I try to live in the country, with the downs at my back and my grandmother's barn owl flapping down the old drove road, bringing home the ghosts I thought I had left my childhood at Glen to escape? My father, who I think likes to say the names of those pockets of land which remain in the family, enjoys drawing up a plan of 'Jacob's Field' where I may build a house of my own. — He loves my son, his favourite grandson: when I throw out my wild plans for the future, he agrees that my son should stay near the River Avon, where the trout rise in the early morning and at dusk and if they're too wily to catch, there's grayling, going up and down to the weir. 'Imber, Imber on the down, seven mile from any town,' chants my father, remembering the jingles of the Edwardian age in which he was reared here, at Wilsford. — A young man, a local councillor, comes to see us at the cottage and suggests renovating the old horse-drawn carriage, which had taken my father, Louis holding the reins, up to the downs with his mother on a jaunt – or to Salisbury, for the first agonising parting at the age of twelve, for Naval College at Dartmouth. But I know I cannot stay here all the time. The neighbouring fantasy concocted by my uncle; the drowsy afternoons by the wild iris beds and the mist from the river once the summer has gone, would drive me back to the city. And there, I have nowhere permanent to live, either. No. 118 Cheyne Walk has been sold, to meet the debts inevitably run up when there is next to nothing coming in. — I am back at 6 Swan Walk; my son is in the room below my girlish bedroom, which is unchanged since I left it in the black car for my first marriage, a lifetime ago. John McCubbin sleeps across the landing from him, an au pair (French) is fitted in somehow; yet it doesn't occur to me then that any of this is inconvenient for my parents. — Luisa comes in to cook, as she had when I was in Cheyne Walk: I am an imperious guest and must have driven my mother mad with my demands and expectations.

As I see now, my long adolescence was in fact the precursor of what, a decade or so later, was to become the norm: postgraduate and night school and diplomas and MAs taking young people well past their youth, without the necessity to settle down or find gainful employment. But I don't believe my parents, even if they sensed this at the time, felt grateful for their role as progenitors of the new trend of postponed maturity. — Just as I am always moving (and Luc with me when he is in England: he seems more temporary than ever now I have no house or flat of my own), so, as I see it now, the balance of my parents' household is disturbed by my mobility – and my father, having slipped a disc, lies several weeks quite still and flat on his back in bed. I go down to the Avon with my son, and with Jon Halliday, the friend of Luc who has become a good friend of mine. — In the train to Salisbury Jon hands me a pamphlet entitled *The Woman Question* by a brilliant young woman he knows, Juliet Mitchell. The slim paper-bound booklet lies in my hand as the train goes deeper into the chalk downs: a faint greyish-green haze lies over the sparsely vegetated heights of the hills and the sky is clear over the woods, ink black at midsummer. 'The woman question?' I ask Jon. For the only question for me is how and where I shall travel next.

All this time, and without my understanding the difference it would make to my life, my father and mother were preparing to leave England for good. They had bought a piece of land by the sea in Corfu, then an island little changed since the days of the Venetians and the French: and in August of that year, 1966, I am in the hotel which until very recently was the only hostelry in the bay of Paleocastritsa, on the west coast of the island. This is the Tourist Pavilion, and along with the new inn, the Living Lobster as it was named, the sole provider of rooms or chips and kebabs for miles around. In this blazing hot summer, in the outdoors restaurant where my father traps wasps with saucers of honey and waiters stagger under grotesquely piled trays, oblivious to our calls, my son is present, as is Peter Eyre, my actor friend – and Luc, who despises this island, with its lush scenery and cypress trees, harking in his mind always to the 'real thing', real beauty, the bare slopes of the Cycladic island where his mother lives and sculpts. Peter is in the Living Lobster, sharing with a dentist who snores and keeps him awake at night; Francis is here too, but staying I think at the Tourist Pavilion, by the edge of a sea he doesn't care to enter much, always reading, even at the hottest time of the day.

We are all here, on this bay which is on the edge of despoliation by tourism, a bay of great beauty, painted by Edward Lear, where Lawrence Durrell has a little house in a neighbouring grove (Luc insists on going to visit him) – we are here because, a short boat ride away, the beach and narrow valley and olive grove which comprise my parents' new life can be found. — The roof of the house my parents have designed for themselves will go on this month; there will be a feast at long tables in the grove; all those who have helped build the house – and us, of course, a band of foreigners – will attend.

Here we are, at the *fête-champêtre* in the grove below my parents' new house. — An uncle of Luc's and his wife Bettina come to appraise the house a few days later; and after doing so they look at me with the incredulity I have come to expect of almost everyone by now: what am I, a 'girl' so much older than my lover? (In those days every year and month were measured, if a woman was older than a man: like a millstone, this age difference in the end wore down the one who carried it, and in most cases ended the relationship, leaving the young man 'free' to marry someone of a suitable age.) Luc's uncle, a dry pseudo-archaeologist, finds the house – white, rectangular, blue-shuttered – too conventional. Bettina, 'artistic' and spiteful-tongued, makes me feel the enmity of Luc's family for mine. — Incredulity turns to laughter and more scorn when the subject of my occupation in London is raised. — And it is true, by answering her questions I am asking for this reaction. For I have left behind me in London all the responsibilities of a small shop, in Elizabeth Street off Ebury Street and not far from my long-suffering parents' house. I have picked up the new fashion for cheap clothes, for tights, for the new democracy and 'classlessness'; I am a little late as ever, but with a friend I am co-owner of a 'boutique'. — My father has put up the £1,500 required to purchase the lease and stock the premises. We have called this unbusinesslike concern the Yellow Room, thus combing the preciosity of my grandmother's generation (Beardsley, Yellow Book, etc.) with the vaguely up-to-date connotations of a 'Room' – Colony Room, Saddle Room – in vogue at the time.

Bettina squints at me, in the grove where my parents have chosen to celebrate their imminent departure from 6 Swan Walk, now piled with my belongings and no sign of my ever moving out, and filled too with unwanted anxiety about my shop, which produces very little in the way of financial return. They will shed all this, along with the constant family scandals and petty worries my father has borne since he came of age. — Little wonder they smile, as sheep turn on the spit high on the hilly land where they have chosen to site their new life. — 'But what on earth do you *sell* there?' rasps Bettina, in the Germanic-French accent which is an imitation of Luc's family's voice: he is part of a world of real artists and writers, and she is not. — I don't know how to tell her, but my father is proud: 'Emma has had a great success, with her caftans . . .' And I squirm. — Why aren't I writing, as I always promised I would do? — Did the débâcle with my one little book at Formentor really put an end to all my hopes? — Now I am someone who drives with my friend, and bolts of brightly coloured furnishing material, to the World's End, to see the dressmaker Mrs Clements in her council flat in Limerston Street. (Charlotte, semi-retired but still a perfectionist with needle and tuck, pleat and gusset, would have been horrified to have been asked to produce these garish garments.) I sell them at seven guineas. But soon they are noticed and copies appear in the windows of major stores. — My son, at least, likes my shop, where stones and rings and oddities can be secured for his museum. Henrietta, the wild woman who transcends girlitude, likes the rail of dresses there, too. — Yet this can't, surely, be all there is to life? I have written whole novels and torn them up or, classically, put them under the bed. But I have moved too often: where is my bed now? The manuscript of one of these novels has vanished for ever. Concerned with the corruption of the world of fashion magazines and advertising, it was entitled *Were You Crying?* I can, I self-pityingly think, ask that question of myself.

The summer in London is long gone by the time I return. It rains and is cold. My son goes away to school, I mind this but his father and his father's family are adamant: besides, what kind of life can I provide for him?— I am now in a studio in Glebe Place, bought on a lease with money left over from the sale of the house. I have painted it *sang-de-boeuf*, a colour of dried blood I have seen in a film by Rossellini on the rise to power of Louis XIV. I concoct a miniature Palace of Fontainebleau – but the repelling nature of the tall dark room with its northern light, and the fact there is a kindergarten outside the tiny window of my equally microscopic bedroom off the studio drives me almost to the point of despair. Children's voices come in all day: I say to myself I can't write in these conditions. — I go to the shop, where necklaces and cheap skirts lie dustily and

Pat, the girl who works there, is in the process of being wooed by a dangerous film star from Amsterdam. — The 'real' Sixties are upon us, and – as Luc is so much away – I pass time with Mick the film-maker, who sits in my studio with his Rizlas and tobacco, and on each visit has longer hair. He likes to play jazz, Coltrane and Thelonious Monk; we lie back on the sofas opposite each other while he talks of going to New York, and of filming his heroes there. But it all begins to seem unreal, an unreality I welcome and understand, in the songs of the Rolling Stones; in the flock of fibreglass sheep, life-size, which stand in Robert Fraser's gallery; in the new drugs which bring new colours, danger and death; people start to die regularly from overdoses – a man known as H dies of his own initial, alone in a boat in the south of France. We all shudder and shiver with a sense of impending catastrophe and rebirth: most of all, demented with sorrow at my own desolation, smug in the sense of my destroyed hopes and my hopeless loves, I listen day and night to the balladeer of the self-obsessed, Bob Dylan.

I am in Chelsea, in Glebe Place, and Luc waits as I pack my bag: I am going out to the island where my parents now are ensconced. Only a few months before, I had waved them goodbye, along with my younger sister Catherine and Toby, my younger brother. Catherine has already developed her re-markable powers, she is one of Nature's intuitive mystics; and, ten years younger than I, she is the one who will guide me, as I become increasingly lost, uncertain of the direction I must follow. Lost? laugh my friends. I can sympathise with Luc when he returns from a film trip and is this time really unable to remember which street we're supposed to be living in. I go round in circles, in the Chelsea streets – with Swan Walk always the epicentre – circles, but to what end? — I have given my father two waste-paper baskets for the new house on Corfu and he smiles, delighted, for his naval neatness will go with him wherever he goes. — My brother and sister and I sat on the window seat in Swan Walk and watched them drive off, car loaded, for an existence that will not involve us.

The train takes us – my son and me – from Victoria across the Channel and then down to Venice, where we shall board a boat filled with German tourists, and will spend two nights on board, before dis-embarking in Corfu. — I know, however, as I set off on this typically complicated and unnecessary journey, that something has ended and there will be worse: shocks and departures, words unspoken which can never now be said. I feel the first pang as we pull out of the station, Luc's figure, as in an old-fashioned movie, growing smaller and then vanishing altogether. The dream of trains and abandonment return that night, in the stuffy sleeper, and is followed by the lake dream, where Luc, distant and still minute, stands on the far side of water. I begin to wish my sister, with her instinctual Jungian know-ledge of behaviour, cause and effect, were here with me on the trip. — But I arrive, happy and apparently self-confident as ever – or, like other girls who find themselves the Peter Pans of their families, over-organised and efficient, belying the core of weakness and indecision inside. — I admire my parents, who have neither electricity nor telephone (though the first will come soon, they seem in no hurry to install a line of communication to the outside world; guiltily I feel they have heard enough of my disasters and prefer to be left in peace). Then comes, on the morning my son and I are due to leave by plane for London, the first wave of the year's horrors. — Martial music sounds on the radio my father likes to listen to before breakfast. The Colonels have seized power. My fear, buried only a few millimetres under the skin, erupts. I dare not fly. Struggling back through Europe and late for the start of my son's term, I sense the dislocation of the world. — London wails with 'A Whiter Shade of Pale'. Alone in the Glebe Place studio I witness the beginnings of the modern world: violence on TV; beautiful violence, in its colours and sounds portraying to a dazed audience of millions the atrocities of the Vietnam War.

Luc stays away on the other side of the globe as 1967 continues to record its filmic fatalities. — Mick comes round, sits with his roll-ups and his neat fingers and talks, or is silent for hours on end. — The last of Luc takes place in his company, when the three of us, that summer, go to Gordes in France. Luc and Mick will film the abstract artist Viktor Vasarely in the beehive-shaped house where he lives, unaffected by the cosmic panic which has gripped the world. The coldness of the geometric planes of his paintings, and the chess set, the size of a whole floor, in another of the ancient shepherd's dwellings the artist has commandeered as his own, only reinforce my sadness. There is a dearth of affect, in the new world we have made for ourselves. Caught in the Snow Queen's domain, longing for a return of feeling, I go back to London, alone with Mick – for to be in his company is to be alone, his mind and perceptions are so unlike mine. — The train, rushing north from Avignon to Paris, carries me further and further from Luc – from what had only ever been a fantasy, a dream.

September winds scatter leaves into the basement flat in East 57th Street which Mick and I are lent by the art critic John Richardson – he and his boyfriend are in the house above: we drink together in the evenings while Mick goes out filming Coltrane or Monk, as he has always wanted to do. I see Dee and other old friends. — But the new mood has descended on New York; he not busy being born is busy dying; and I am rootless, blown in the wind that is the song which sounds from every all-night store in Dee's Greenwich Village district. — I have to go back: there is nothing for me to do here and this is the worst place on earth to have nothing to do. Mick is happy: he has found Val, a black girl who is, for him, the epitome of the depravity and excitement of Manhattan. When I finally leave, Mick is too stoned to hear me say I'm on my way.

MICK THE FILM-MAKER

An Interlude

It was some months before I saw Mick again. I was back in my studio, lonely and wishing for Luc; but Mick, as so often before, was what I got: and one evening we went off to have a drink together. He chose a pub near where he lived – Earls Court – and ordered a glass of red wine and sat playing with the stem of the glass just as he had done when I last saw him in New York. Otherwise he looked haggard, and older; his long hair had been chopped off above the ears and there was a small hole in his left earlobe where his golden ring had hung.

'It's impossible,' he said. 'I couldn't carry the weight any longer. What's so terrible is the loneliness. You're sitting with Val and you know you're not there. Her eyes . . . she's not taking anything in any more. Last summer she got better, we even went for a country holiday and she swam in the stream. What life she's got in there somewhere! She dived in and out like a kingfisher. It was extraordinary. Now she doesn't care who she goes after so long as she gets the stuff. People she doesn't know . . . film people . . . and she's taking dresses off rails and walking away with them as if she doesn't care whether she's caught or not. I gave up. I just had to.'

'What about the film?' I said. When I had left Mick in the States he had asked me to help with the script of what was going to be his first feature film. In those days words like 'bi-lateral' and 'parameter' were thrown about when describing as yet unrealised works and I'd never been too clear what the subject was. It seemed an American producer had liked Mick's documentaries and had asked him to make a film about his life. Val was going to be the star, a black girl from Manhattan who meets Mick and cuts across his conventional, uptight life, changing his lifestyle and his outlook and exploding on to the screen in a galaxy of psychedelic colour and Jimi Hendrix. Mick asked me to write the kind of dialogue he had used before the great revelation; he and Val would improvise the rest. It was hard to imagine that all this could be spun out to last ninety minutes – but in the event I didn't stay long enough to find out.

Back in London the idea was revived. The script meetings were chaotic, with Val dancing about rolling joints and Mick's eyes fixed on her in adoration, no concrete idea in his head. The money kept being delayed too, and Mick's phone and electricity were frequently cut off. They had a lodger, Andy, who came in late at night and ate the dog's food out of its bowl in the dark. Already the Sixties dream of limitless funds and 'projects' was turning sour and I began to suspect the film would never come off. I needed to earn my living, and one day I didn't turn up at the first-floor Earls Court flat where the big central room had a four-poster bed built by Mick and a stereo and nothing else. He called me once from a phone box and then there was silence. 'I'm working on it now,' Mick said. He stopped stroking the stem of his wine glass and began to roll a cigarette. He had thin, delicate fingers. When he leant forward his shoulders were narrower than before he'd gone away. His face had a deep-frozen look, as if his successful, self-consciously carefree youth had been preserved behind the lines of anxiety and guilt. 'We've got a new backer. He's a merchant banker, but he's together. There's no problem with funding. It'll be a great movie. I needed the time for the whole concept to settle down. Hey, why don't you join us?' Then he sighed. 'He hasn't seen Val yet. It's her part, there's no doubt about that. I couldn't let anyone else even look at it. Well, think what Val did for me. She set me free. OK, she needed me to help her . . . find work, get herself together . . . what a background she comes from, you know? The first three months I was with her I didn't even try to fuck her. If you've been doing it standing up against a wall since you were eleven years old you don't need some ofay cat to come along and tell you what to do. No, Mick and Val could have been happy for a very long time, I can tell you that.'

The pub was beginning to fill up. Mick had hardly tasted his drink. He drained the glass suddenly and went over to the bar for more. When he came back two Jamaican men and a girl had come in and he relapsed into his native English. He had once told me of a strict upbringing with a widowed schoolteacher mother, and when under strain the remnants of his childhood language broke through the cool. 'I have to keep in touch with her, of course. What I really need is to get away from it all. Perhaps I'd be able to see it in perspective if I got away. Am I to blame for what's happened? I live round the corner from the old flat. So you can't say Val and I have really parted. We're in striking distance of each other. But you remember what she was like when she was in New York, don't you? Quite incredible.'

'Yes, I remember,' I said.

'The energy! She was like an electric current. People like that have to burn themselves up, maybe. You'd think that she'd have been offered work. And nothing! That's why the film's so important. It'll make her name. I don't care about me. But I told her she'll really have to pull herself together when she meets him. Get a grip, I mean.'

Mick fell silent. I saw there was no use trying to talk to him, his eyes were looking inward as he endlessly replayed the reel of his and Val's life together. For a time I thought of Val too. She had certainly attracted attention in the fringe rock play off off-Broadway, where she had danced on to the stage in a red dress and shimmered like summer lightning in front of an audience of hippies and anarchists and smart critics ready to give her a careful rave in the papers next day. When the fuss had died down she tried to become a model, but very few black girls made it to the top, then. She had drifted, presumably, into unemployment and drugs. I tried to imagine her now, shattered and slow-moving and hollow-eyed, and failed.

'She won't last long at this rate,' he said. 'The trouble is, I'm responsible. If I didn't have to keep in touch I could get away and concentrate on the film.'

Mick rose and drained off his second glass. I finished my drink and we left the pub. He walked down the Earls Court Road with head down and shoulders bowed as all the different races of the world streamed past us. I felt he had understood something – that he and his kind were responsible for all the suffering that had ever taken place on the face of the earth – and that the responsibility was driving him mad. I left him on the corner. He said he was going to stand there a while and see if Val passed. She sometimes got herself to go out by evening, he said.

When I saw Mick again it was in another part of London. Two months had passed, there was a heat-wave, and in the busy market I used to visit on Saturdays he stood out very white against the bare brown arms and legs and garish cottons of the Portobello Road tourists. He was wearing a faded denim jacket and pants, and his fair hair seemed to have faded too; a pale stubble covered his face. He came up to me and took hold of my arm just above the elbow. 'I'm going away for a couple of weeks. I don't know how she'll manage. I need the bread. Andy put me on to it. But I look like someone they'd stop, don't I?' He laughed. 'I came here to the market to buy a straight suit. Where's the old clothes bit? Under the bridge, isn't it?' We moved up the market in pursuit of a straight suit. I remembered that Andy, the one-time eater of dog food in Mick's flat, had been trying to set up a documentary on the Mafia in the Aspromonte mountains for French TV. Pre-sumably he had fixed a dangerous job for Mick – a job like getting an interview with a contact, to set up the programme. I wondered what kind of film Mick had told Val he was making.

In front of a rack of dark grey suits that looked as if they had done service at funerals twenty years before and been exposed to the weather ever since, Mick paused and fingered the threadbare material.

'This'll do. It takes me back to my prep school.' He pulled a face. 'Like, were those terrible days. Wow!' He looked brighter as he spoke the jargon of the Sixties and smiled as he tried on the jacket. It was pinched at the shoulders, giving him the air of an old little boy. 'I'll take it. Two quid. Not bad. Hey, you couldn't lay two quid on me, could you? Thanks. Did I tell you we're really getting the script together now? It's the American again. He said he couldn't get the images out of his head. Money's easier now. There's a boom coming. I won't try on the pants. What're you doing now? You ought to come in on my movie. I'd like you to be in it. If I come back from this trip alive, that is.'

We left the market and walked up towards the library. Mick seemed pleased with his suit. But as we parted his face fell and his eyes looked inward again. 'She's worse than ever now, you know. Hallucinations. She thought she saw a man – a guy she got mixed up with in New York. He's a killer. He's in San Quentin now. For life. He can't be here. He got hold of her when she was eleven years old. Well, whatever happens to me I don't know who'll get hold of her when I'm away. She doesn't care what she does these days.'

Before I had time to wish him luck Mick had stepped backwards off the library steps, turned and was walking fast towards the main road and the shops. 'Haircut and shave,' he shouted over his shoulder. He held up the suit and grinned. I watched him go into a barber's shop, and thought of him at the Mafia-guarded Naples airport – a small, unconvincing 'English businessman' sweating in fear of being gunned down by the Cosa Nostra in a grey flannel suit.

A few days later I was lying on my bed reading and trying to get cool when the phone rang and it was Val. I knew her voice although I hadn't heard it for two years: fast and low-pitched in a stream of words that seemed to have no connection until it hit you when she paused to draw breath that she was trying to put over several layers of meaning at once and in an odd way succeeding. Even when Val was at her most incomprehensible a sort of atmosphere came off her speech. It was like watching a speeded-up film and making what sense you could of the flashing pictures and sounds. This time, in comparison to the past, she was short and to the point. 'Money. What I mean is like I need money now and if you come over you c'd give it to me here. OK? Is that OK with you?'

I guessed Mick had left my phone number before he left 'on location'. Val's voice was slightly cracked; otherwise she sounded as energetic as she had in New York. I paused, holding the phone. It was hot outside and I didn't much want to go through the crowds of Chelsea into the crowds of Earls Court. 'Duff's here. He wants to say hello, and how's Luc?' I flinched; for junkies, time stands still. 'And Andy. Steve's here, he says £10 would've been OK a year ago, now we better have twenty. Oh Rocky, will you get off my leg? Where's Hai Kee? What food? Why she have to go out for food?' The phone at Val's end crashed down. I got up after a few minutes, had a cold shower and changed my clothes, then went out into the blazing light. It seemed to take a long time to get to Earls Court. The tourist season had begun and I pushed my way through groups of mutually uncomprehending people to get to the door of Mick's flat. I thought things would be no better between Val and myself than they were with the foreigners in the street: Mick had once told me she couldn't understand a word I said either.

The bell was grimy. A loud male voice shouted down the intercom. 'You come with the bread? Come up. Door's open.'

As soon as I walked into the big room in the flat I remembered the last time I had been there, Mick's last party. Duff had been there too – he was a playwright who Luc had tried to film, unsuccessfully, and he was running round the room banging his head against the walls. Dark red wine slopped from his glass on to the bare boards. He was shouting and roaring. Steve too: an English imitator of Jim Dine, small and frail, with a disused garage in south London filled with brightly painted wire clippers and garden shears. Then, some of his works had been on the walls at Mick's. I remembered a painting of a window, with a blue sky and a neat suburban garden outside, and a real shelf jutting out into the room with a toilet roll on it, and a set of yellow kitchen utensils hooked on to a canvas. Now the walls were empty again. Duff and Steve were sitting quietly on the floor at the far end of the room. A tiny board was between them: it could have been chess or backgammon. Andy was lying in his usual position, on a pile of dusty bedding, too tired to look up or wave when I came in. I skirted him and went over to the four-poster bed.

Val was stretched out on the purple velvet coverlet.

Her tight black jeans went down into high red boots that looked as if they had been sprayed on to her legs. The bottom half of her body was immobile, but from the waist up she gyrated. The music was Aretha Franklin. I thought of the time when work on the film was interrupted by Jimi Hendrix's visit to London. He'd stayed in the hotel opposite the flat. His overflow costumes had been housed by Val in the big cupboards in the hall. Sara, Val's friend, opened the cupboards every five minutes to look inside.

Val's face was thinner and her eyes were shining very bright. 'Hi-i. You know like I was in the *park* yesterday and they got these new kites I guess if you're an air sign you can go up there with them. What's that? I can't count money, Duff this isn't English twenty, looks like a couple of blues. OK it'll do. I bought a little dog today. You r'member that dog we used to have? He died same month as everyone else. So we waited all this time and we went and bought the little champ he's pedigree isn't that right champ?'

Val pulled back the coverlet. A tiny dog was buried in the blankets. It looked like a rat that had had a dog's skin stitched on to it. Duff laughed and came over. '*Bought*. Val just picked that animal out of the straw. She put it under her coat. It freaked out when we had to walk through the record department.' 'It bit me,' Val said. She lifted her shirt and we stared at the neat wound under her right breast. 'Harrods is best for dogs. What else did I do, Duff?'

'So Mick's gone,' I said. Duff had wandered back to his game with Steven. 'How long'll he be away on his trip . . . ?' While I spoke I looked over at Duff again. There was something about Mick and Val's flat that seemed to drain the life out of people. He wasn't writing plays any more. Steve saw me watching and gave a ghostly smile. I wondered if he was painting. He gave the impression of having been sitting on the floor of Mick's flat longer than Duff – as long as Andy, almost.

'Who?' Val slid off the bed and held the two £5 notes out in Andy's direction. 'Go on, Andy. Don't be long. You wanna take Champ with you he needs some air?'

'I'm not taking Champ,' Andy mumbled. He got up very slowly and shuffled to the door, dragging strips of bedding across the floor as he went. 'See ya.' The door of the flat banged behind him.

'See ya later.' Val was standing in the middle of the room, still swaying to the music. I had forgotten how tall she was, and the high red boots made her taller. Her legs and slim hips were like the stalk of a long flower, the surprisingly full breasts, thick black hair and gleaming face an exotic blossom in the bare room. She seemed happy. I thought of Mick, the lines of anxiety etched into his pale face. There was little trace of him here, apart from the bed he had painstakingly made. It occurred to me she didn't even know he'd gone.

'Mi-ick.' She danced over towards Duff and Steven and back again. 'The creep didn't leave me any bread. Am I s'posed to starve? And Champ needs steak that's what these pedigrees are used to. After Andy's back shall we go to the park again? Shall we, Champ? I might send him up in a kite wouldn't that be wild.' She came up close to me, as if trying to find some way in which we could communicate. 'You wanna come to the park? I saw a guy there yesterday I useta know when I was a kid. Mick said I wasn't to talk to him. You can come and see me not talk to him.' She laughed. At the same time her cheeks drooped and her eyes went dead, I saw the pupils go up under the lids. I put my arms forward to catch her. But she didn't fall. 'Andy's taking a long time.' Her voice was slurred. 'Duff come next door with me, will ya.'

There was a cell next to the big room. Andy slept there. Duff got up from the floor and came to put his arms round Val. He led her out to the cell. Steven was leaning against the wall now, with his eyes shut. Only the tiny dog glared at me as I went over to the door. I had the feeling there wasn't very much point in waiting for Val to appear again. I shouted goodbye at the top of the stairs.

'See ya later.' Val's voice had the same cracked sound as when she phoned me, but there was still an amazing amount of energy in it. I only realised how tiring it was in the flat when I left it, and made my way through the evening crowds of Earls Court.

A few weeks later, my bell at the studio rang at eleven o'clock at night. Mick didn't ask if this was a good time to come round. He went ahead of me into the sitting-room and sat on a straight-backed chair, spurning the sofa and the cushions. 'I had a shit-awful time in Calabria. I was away a month in the end. I thought God knows what might have happened to her. What? No, you'd think no one had ever heard of the Mafia. I was going to use the money Andy promised me to go away with Val and get her better and write the script for the film. Just my luck I picked the wrong village – an identical one, mind you, to the one I was told to dig around in.' He dug in his jeans pocket and came out empty-handed. 'You haven't got a roll-up, have you? OK, I'll take one of those.'

I saw his hand was shaking. His face was gaunt, and yellow from the sun of the past months. He looked like bad luck. I remembered the cheeky, 'lucky' young director of the avant-garde documentary on Victor Vasarely. Everything had been going for him then. 'Val's worse than ever. I've moved back in. She just can't manage on her own.' He sighed and puffed smoke. 'The money would've helped. But this American producer's still keen. All he wants is a synopsis and we're ready to start.'

I was surprised on two scores and couldn't help showing it. 'You mean you haven't even written the synopsis yet? I thought you wrote that in New York?' Mick shrugged. I knew it was tactless but I went on: 'I went and saw Val when you were away, you know. I could see she was . . . on something, but she didn't seem as bad as all that.'

Mick sat up even straighter in the chair. I saw then that his whole body was completely tense; the hand holding the cigarette shook painfully. 'It's not just that. This guy Val was once mixed up with is here in London. He's dangerous. He wrecked her life, you know. I have to make sure she doesn't get to see him.'

'But I thought you said he was in San Quentin.' For

some reason I couldn't help going on like this, blowing all Mick's covers. But I was beginning to feel afraid. His eyes were staring into the distance as if I wasn't there at all. I suddenly wished he would go.

'No he's here all right. Mind you, I don't know how he escaped from that place. He got Life; that's the odd thing about the whole business.' Mick reached for another cigarette. 'I didn't believe he was here at first. Then I saw him too.' He got up. 'You couldn't spare the pack, could you? Thanks. Look, you really must get involved in the film again. I'm doing a new synopsis, we had to scrap the old one. If Val was well enough I'd have the thing written by the end of the week.'

I went with him to the door. 'Why did you scrap the old one? You were pleased with it, weren't you?'

'Sure,' Mick smiled, more to himself than at me. 'So many things have changed. So many people died. I'd still like you to do that dialogue. I'll call you next week. It's a great part for Val, I wouldn't give it to anyone else. See you then.'

But I didn't see Mick again.

ELEVEN

Revolution Now!

Alexander Cockburn, 1969

'Don't go to a pub with Claud Cockburn. He'll make you pay for the drinks.' Henry Green, my ex-father-in-law, is in his half-landing den, it is raining outside and the rain has intensified the smell of gin, which must now have marinated the little room so thoroughly that even Dig's most strenuous efforts will not be able to get it out. — Dig herself, after letting me into a hall laid to carpet as their smaller house in Trevor Square had been, in black-and-white squares of Axminster or Wilton, giving the same surreal, slightly off-balance effect, has disappeared into the drawing-room. I see her in my mind's eye, dusting the lampshade under the portrait of Henry – though as far as I know, she didn't clean or cook, these services being performed by a Spaniard, usually male. — Henry is shaking his head and looking lugubrious; then comes the high-pitched cackle of laughter. He is enjoying the thought of my coming penury at the hands of Claud Cockburn, once founder of the scabrous publication *The Week*, scourge of 'The Cliveden Set', as he named a group of high-born and rich Nazi sympathisers in Britain; a writer and journalist now retired to Ireland with his wife, Patricia. — For a moment, Henry and I have both forgotten that it was to Henry's son that I was married, and not to him; and that it is Claud and not Claud's son who must on no account be trusted over a pint in the pub. — Henry, I believe, has no intention of taking in the existence of a further generation in any case. His enjoyment here lies, as ever, in the possibility of my discomfiture. 'Gone too far?' he whinnies up at me. I haven't been asked to take a seat and indeed there isn't one, as a malfunctioning TV takes up the only other chair in the den. I can't help recalling that the Anglo-Irish mistress of the 'big house' in Henry's masterpiece *Loving* is called Mrs Tennant. Possibly Henry's contempt for my father and our family runs deep.

Claud's son Alexander is indeed the member of the Cockburn family with which I am now involved. — Raised in Ireland, near Cork, in a house not far removed from the mansion envisaged by Henry in his novel, he has the strong radical sympathies of his father – but, since Hungary and other discovered horrors of the Soviet regime have rendered old-style communism less than palatable, he has allied himself with the most recent development in Socialist thought, the *New Left Review*. ('New Left?' jokes a friend from my rotunda days on hearing of my new enthusiasm for the 'Festive Marxism' I am promised by articles in this hitherto-unknown-to-me organ; 'it's the only *new* thing left.') — However that may be, I am proud of my discovery. As usual I am a little late, as these handsome – and generally middle-class – editors of the *Review* are already invited to sit on panels and appear on TV. The Revolution is on its way: students are rising up against their professors; a whole generation of disaffected, highly pampered young people are on the move. — This is perfect for me; and perhaps my ex-father-in-law sees this, as he chuckles over my irritation at his remark about paying for Claud's drink. Henry is – as anyone can see who is not entirely, as I was, preoccupied with themselves – still as clever as he was in his days of writing and receiving praise for his work: he only appears, now, a drunkard, too deaf to take in the present world. For, of course, what Henry is telling me is that Claud and Claud's kind think nothing of breaking eggs in order to make their particular brand of omelette. And, unkind and perspicacious, Henry has seen at once that I, in this scenario, will be the egg. — Added to which, I shall, of course, be expected to pay for the drinks.

None of this is in my mind, on this fine day in May 1968 when marching down a long boulevard (I can't remember which but I do know it is too long, and a tribute to Haussmann's genius with his reconstruction of nineteenth-century Paris which swept away the narrow thoroughfares and cobbles so useful for throwing at figures of authority, replacing these with the wide avenues which give me, at this agonising moment, extremely painful feet). — I must find a shoe shop. It is irritating to lose one's place in the march – but my companion (this is what I must call Claud's son: boyfriend has gone, lover is out of the question, fiancé laughable; I am training myself, after a visit to Cuba earlier in the year, to refer to him, as some of the erstwhile girls – now women – living with radicals do, as 'compañero') — Alexander, in any case, is happy for me to try on shoes while the world marches by. — The trouble is, I want smart shoes. — We are still in a *banlieue*. I select in the end a pair of brown brogues, covered with fancy holes and laces. We are both downcast by their huge price, and equally by the hugeness of my feet once in them. —

209

The pain doesn't abate, as we continue on our furious rally to St-Germain and the Sorbonne.

It is a few months since I have been affiliated to the New Left (this affiliation occurring more in my mind than anywhere else: women, for all their early struggles against male supremacy, find the hardest battle is against those very radicals who should welcome their emancipation. No one has asked me to attend a meeting or contribute an idea. I was the only one to pay my own ticket on the rackety plane, carrier of Eric Hobsbawm, Robin Blackburn, Ken Coates and the like to Havana. But I expected this attitude, and if I feel a *frisson* of satire days, I conceal my apprehension, even when Claud is taken on by *Private Eye* for a column). — In these few months I have also concealed my surprise at having co-existed, as I now see, alongside a whole new world, a language and a culture I had no idea was there. — The works of Walter Benjamin are now known to me – even if incomprehensible in many aspects, they provide the notion of a 'bourgeoisie', a word now becoming as popular as the yo-yo in previous days, of 'underdevelopment' (like most people in Britain I was taken unawares by the new lingo: – I had thought a film much liked by *New Left Review* contributors, *Memories of Underdevelopment*, had as its subject the problems of a starlet suffering from too-small breasts) and 'solidarity' (the room proclaiming it was dedicated to 'Solidaridad' in the requisitioned Hilton Hotel in Havana had baffled me for days). — Before coming to Paris I had gone to Brussels to stay with Fred Warner, once a simple travelling companion and ex-proposee, now a capitalist (another new word: I don't recall my father ever using the term though he must have been a wonderful example to Claud and his son). Fred has spoken gravely of eggs and omelettes and advised me not to go to the seedbed of Revolution. — I realised, I believe, at that point, that any earlier fondness for Guy Burgess in his past had not actually been of the Bolshevik description: this enabled me, I am ashamed to confess, to decide I disapproved of this kind-hearted man, whose main aim on my visit to the capital of a country of capitalists was to take me to an expensive restaurant and order me the Belgian speciality, Waterzooi. — But I am too excited, as we finally reach the end of the boulevard and see the radical chic of St Germain looming ahead, too in love with the rhetoric and the glory of Revolution, to care.

What I was least able to understand, in Paris in that May of 1968, was the attitude of older people – of the *bourgeoisie*, naturally – who disapproved of the activities of the young. — Nancy Mitford, with whom I had been so frequently – and mindlessly – compared, speaks on TV from her home in Versailles, or a genteel suburb nearby: she fears all the '*bien-pensants*' of her neighbourhood thoroughly dislike the students and wishes life to go on as it had before. — But it is so obviously improved now. All the questions are being asked of authority which, for longer than any of us had been alive, had gone unanswered. — So I, and thousands like me, believed;

though it is harder, now, to look back with absolute understanding on those heady days. — There were so many young people in the streets (it was this, perhaps, which made for an absence of clear thinking) that the prospect of the Revolution's ultimate failure was unacceptable. — The fact I was a girl of thirty myself made my belief in the new 'freedom' all the more doubtful. I clung perhaps, to the hope that this wave of youth would, paradoxically, remove my status of permanent girlhood and allow me to become a woman. — However that may be, two white heads at the Odéon bolster the faith of my companion and myself. They are the heads of Stephen Spender and Mary McCarthy, come to Paris to witness the second French Revolution; and, being by far the oldest members of the audience, they appear very likely to have been present at the first. — The young men, indistinguishable from Danton or Camille Moulins, who climb the podium, charm the poet, as well as his friend and the self-conscious revolutionaries, Alexander and myself. — But my *compañero* is so strikingly handsome (Cecil Beaton, to whom I have introduced him in London, has remarked on the close resemblance to Rupert Brooke, 'the handsomest young man in England') that we forget for a moment, as we throng the Odéon steps, that we are at the beginning of a new democratic order and not at a party in Hampstead or Kensington. Spender compounds this sensation by assuring us as we walk by his side through festive Marxists, Trotskyists and Leninists, workers (few of these) and a mass of undetermined other sectarians, that his hosts, the French Rothschilds, are eating only

hard-boiled eggs throughout these stirring times. —
We walk on, to the rue St-Sévérin, where we have a
room not far from the falling trees and burning cars
of this new Paris, and we go out again, to the Joie de
Lire, to buy Althusser, Barthes, Fanon and Foucault:
I understand very little of these, and my comrade,
who makes light of his role as an intellectual of the
New Left Review brigade, seems to grasp them as
little as I, in the original French at least. — We return,
we sleep briefly, we go out to march and, as is
inevitable on such occasions, I find myself alone as in
a nightmare, chased across the cobbles at the
Sorbonne by police wielding canisters of tear gas . . .
At the Beaux Arts we buy posters; in the rue de
l'Ancienne Comédie we go as tourists to Voltaire's
eating place. How could the city of Oscar Wilde and
the moribund wallpaper have seemed so exciting to
me? What do I care, breaking off from the painful
shouting and banner-waving of St-Germain, for the
walled gardens of the rue Jacob, with the Temple de
l'Amitié, once a place of pilgrimage for me, the shrine
to the ideal of friendship rather than love which I had
decided to espouse, this erected by Natalie Clifford
Barney for her friend the lesbian Princesse de
Polignac? — I care for none of it. — There will be
little money to live on when we get home, but the
Revolution will provide.

In London I discover I am pregnant. My son will be
ten years old when the child is born, but he is
delighted, and I, at last – or so I believe – I shall
combine the uncombinable: Revolution and Stability.
We move – where else? – back to Swan Walk. The
house has been made over to my younger brother,

but he has no need of it yet, and I feel I am in a museum – with the return, when they come from their house and family in Battersea, of John McCubbin and Luisa – and the furniture, plates and cups and saucers of my parents who wished perhaps to make sure their move to a Greek island was a happy one before emptying their nest at home. — But their home really is there and we stay, untroubled by the need to move – for now – while I await the birth. — We must marry; so, surprisingly, that ancient revolutionary Claud Cockburn says; and so, after we have visited them in Ireland in the summer of 1968, and after waiting so long that only a Chinese tunic of Patricia's will fit my burgeoning form, we do.

Claud and Patricia at this time live near Youghal, in County Cork. I am astonished there, by leaking roof and swaying banister; by Claud's greatly etiolated limbs and husky bronchial cough. — I love and am charmed by him instantly. — I see his wife hide his whisky in the grandfather clock in the hall; and, wickedly, I creep out to retrieve it for him. — Claud's anecdotes are his treasury: he counts them out and his own laugh precedes one's own and comes, sometimes, long before the end of the story. — The Woodbines burn in fingers stained dark brown. — In the pub in Youghal, he dictates his column for the *Irish Times* in the phone box and is helped up and down from the decaying leather bench by his sons, of whom he has three. — It comes to me that I want only to belong to other families, and that I like this one. — But, with my son, I must return like Goldilocks to the house my parents have deserted and eat their porridge with their silver spoons. No hint of responsibility has entered the ménage, either through the father of my future child, or, despite being older than he is, the pregnant thirty-one-year-old who will go to King's College Hospital within a couple of months to have another child. — For this, as I am dismally reminded that I am close to the age when Jesus Christ left this life, is what I now am. And I have done a very great deal less than he.

The wedding, in the same drawing-room overlooking the river as the reception given by my parents for my last marriage, lacks their presence. The Revolutionaries stand around, well pleased with the furniture and good pictures and china in the house. But there is a difference from a few years before: in the little study behind the drawing-room a group of silent young people, friends of my sister, sit hunched and contemplative: not one of them holds a glass and I reel back from the smell of marijuana. — But, again, there are no parental figures to be shocked – not that they would have been, I dare say; but my need for them, in this changed life as a superannuated girl with no one to shock or please, makes me at that moment miss them more than I had thought I could do. — The Sixties are winding up, and their victims or celebrants winding down, in the room where my father stuck the last pieces of the Gothic castle he made for my sister in the room below the dressing-room where the family of kittens played after John's sudden vanishing from the scene. — But things are also much the same. A Marxist-Leninist passes out cold in the drawing-room, overfed with Old-Fashioneds. My new sister-in-law, the pipe-smoking daughter of Claud and Jean Ross (model for Isherwood's Sally Bowles) dances over my prone and vast body as I, too, collapse on the floor of my parents' home. We are all having a wonderful time.

In hospital in early February 1969, I am called by a friend from the *New Left Review*. (This is what he is, a friend and not a colleague; I have come to understand that I and other *compañeras* of the New Left will never be included in the deliberations of these architects of a True Socialist Future.) My friend is Peter Wollen, whose companion and future wife is Laura Mulvey, clever and dark-haired, of whom I am very fond. They expect a child in three or four months. 'What have you had? asks Peter, as I lie in the room at the end of the ward, a resolutely no-pink-trimmed crib by my side. I hear my fatuous answer and blush, yet it's too late to go back and certainly impossible to contradict. 'A woman,' I reply, realising the extent of my indoctrination to the new era's correctness, and also my own miserable failure at learning the lessons from *The Woman Question*, the pamphlet which a friend had pressed into my hand in the days before the world changed.

If I have given birth to a woman, I ponder afterwards, can I at last give up being a girl?